Node.js for Embedded Systems

Using Web Technologies to
Build Connected Devices

Patrick Mulder and Kelsey Breseman

Beijing · Boston · Farnham · Sebastopol · Tokyo

Node.js for Embedded Systems

by Patrick Mulder and Kelsey Breseman

Printed in the United States of America.

Published by O'Reilly Media, Inc., 1005 Gravenstein Highway North, Sebastopol, CA 95472.

O'Reilly books may be purchased for educational, business, or sales promotional use. Online editions are also available for most titles (*http://safaribooksonline.com*). For more information, contact our corporate/institutional sales department: 800-998-9938 or *corporate@oreilly.com*.

Editors: Nan Barber and Susan Conant	**Indexer:** WordCo Indexing Services, Inc.
Production Editor: Colleen Cole	**Interior Designer:** David Futato
Copyeditor: Jasmine Kwityn	**Cover Designer:** Karen Montgomery
Proofreader: Christina Edwards	**Illustrator:** Rebecca Demarest

October 2016:   First Edition

Revision History for the First Edition
2016-10-06:   First Release

See *http://oreilly.com/catalog/errata.csp?isbn=9781491928998* for release details.

978-1-491-92899-8

[LSI]

Table of Contents

Foreword

It is a wonderful time to be playing with physical computing!

In the early 2000s, there were few options for any given physical computing technology. If you wanted to measure humidity you had one option—with the annoying subtleties of that particular manufacturer. Thanks to the pressure of free market forces and open source hardware, by the mid-2010s there were dozens of manufacturers all creating similar humidity sensors. The pinouts were identical, the protocols were identical (and finally standardized to I2C), and the prices were falling. Today I don't have to wonder if the sensor came from silicon foundry X or Y, I just have to decide "do I want to measure the humidity inside my lunchbox?" I plug in whatever humidity sensor is most readily available and let the library handle the necessary low-level interactions to get the data. I am no longer worrying about the underlying hardware; I can instead concentrate on the user experience.

The user experience is central to the popularity of Arduino. Its simplified interface enabled the crashing of two worlds: designers and engineers. Similarly, the JavaScript and the Node.js ecosystem are easy to learn for designers and non-professional programmers. In the future the mindset of designers and users of hardware will matter more than who holds the keys to building electronics. Thanks to the Web, baseline tools (gcc, serial bootloaders, skillet reflow, etc.) are universal and now easy to master. Anyone with a hot plate and a pair of tweezers can begin making small batches of products that connect to the Internet. And thanks to the Web we can market and sell all manner of devices across the globe.

A base-level microcontroller is now ambiguous between manufacturers. Does it have serial, I2C, SPI? Does it have multichannel ADCs? Does it have good low-power performance? Is it cheap and readily available? Can I program it with the industry's standard toolchain? Nearly every microcontroller on the market satisfies these requirements. Microcontroller manufacturers are now having to develop advancements on the fringes: Does it come with BLE and WiFi? Can I reprogram it over-the-air?

The hardware industry will continue to jam more processing power into smaller spaces, with inconceivable amounts of storage and connectivity. I'm not sure where we will end this next decade, but it's clear that specific chip manufacturers will begin to look like the DEC and Tandy computers of the 1980s: no one cared about the hardware inside their computer; they just wanted their spreadsheet to open. Thankfully, advancements in open source software are continuing to push what us regular folks can do. Node.js and JavaScript in the browser make it possible for the vast majority of folks to move up the toolchain. I can stop worrying about whether my serial buffer is going to overrun and concentrate on the bigger picture.

I dream of the day that I can purchase a clock, a desk lamp, or a wristwatch and configure its interactions the way I want them. I should be able to plug a USB cable into a consumer product and have a known set of inputs and outputs. The compiler, or whatever it becomes, should warn me when I'm doing something wrong (but allow me to do it anyway :). These new tools increase the leverage we have over hardware. But we should all remember it's not the hardware, it's how you use it. Let's hope better tools enable us to build things that matter.

— Nathan Seidle
Founder, SparkFun Electronics
TEDx Speaker on Open Source Business

Preface

This book describes the role that JavaScript plays in embedded devices. Driven by Arduino and Raspberry Pi, there is an ongoing democratization of hardware development processes. New boards and software toolchains make hardware development more accessible, the same way full stack JavaScript's usability made programming easier to approach.

Inspired by open feedback and worldwide collaboration, there are evolving communities on the Web where people join hands to build weather stations, robots, or spectrometers (for a nice overview of this trend, see the entries for the 2015 Hackaday Prize (*https://hackaday.io/submissions/prize2015/list*)).

Compared to those "hobby" projects, professional hardware development often comes with high costs of special computer-aided design (CAD) software products or additional toolchains. This is very different from web development, where the free and open source tools hobbyists use to build are often the same tools used by professionals. In open source software, the lines frequently blur between the work of professional and hobbyist: thousands of examples can be found on GitHub, where many software developers (often joined by "hobbyists") build solutions for business or private needs.

The Arduino and Raspberry Pi ecosystems already heavily depend on open source projects hosted on GitHub. But for building embedded systems, GitHub is not a complete solution because it is not built for collaboration on hardware, and change detection between revisions of a hardware board can be very messy. (There are web collaboration platforms specifically designed for building open source hardware, including Upverter (*https://upverter.com*) and Autodesk Circuits (*https://circuits.io*); however, these platforms are in very early stages and not yet ready for primetime).

GitHub is not the only place where you can find the ingredients to embedded systems with JavaScript. You can also turn to Hackster.io (*https://hackster.io*) (where you can post projects and compare your design with those created by other members), or OSH Park (*https://oshpark.com*) and Tindie (*https://www.tindie.com*) (where you can find ideas to assemble circuits or buy—and sell—directly from and to other makers). In addition, companies such as Seeed Studio, SparkFun, Adafruit, Amazon, and eBay offer a variety of kits and ready-made devices. If you are stuck with building hardware, you can find instructional videos on YouTube or Vimeo about basic and advanced electronics.

When building hardware, you also need some special equipment to solder, laser cut, or 3D print objects. Fab Labs are one solution to this problem. Fab Labs are low-cost fabrication laboratories (hence the name "Fab Lab") where you can rent equipment to print, assemble, and debug hardware for your own needs. (Neil Gershenfeld from MIT is one of the main inventors of Fab Labs. Watch his talk (*https://www.ted.com/ talks/neil_gershenfeld_on_fab_labs*) to find out more.) It is amazing to see how blueprints from the Internet can transform into physical objects in a Fab Lab. It is equally amazing to see how your hardware skills and know-how will evolve if you visit a Maker space regularly.

No doubt, building hardware can be fun. But much of the secret sauce in embedded development is in the software—and this is where the opportunity for JavaScript developers arises. Because they are already familiar with the importance of events, interactions, and user experience, JavaScript developers can potentially build physical experiences with embedded devices that feel more natural and human than similar experiences with other languages.

To achieve this goal, a prospective embedded developer must master elements from both web technologies and robotics. In web technologies, you will need skills such as JavaScript, CSS, and SVG to build graphical user interfaces for devices, as well as web servers and protocols to manage communication across networks. On the physical side, you need to understand the different approaches for controlling physical systems and robots themselves.

JavaScript will play a major role in a more connected society because JavaScript is *the* programming language for the Web. Once you become comfortable with its asynchronous programming model, you'll find that JavaScript offers elegant solutions to dealing with data and functions in networks and embedded systems too.

In addition to JavaScript and web technologies, this book will touch on some ideas about electronic circuits and their applications to the Internet of Things (IoT). There are other books that are much more focused on how to build these types of products, but this book provides a starting point.

It won't be too long before we will be using web browsers to monitor traffic in a city, the contents of a warehouse, or progress from a personal workout where data is captured from sensors in clothes. And, of course, building these systems makes sense only if we can share the results with friends, colleagues, and peers. As embedded developers for the web, you're on the leading edge, inventing this new world.

If you've worked with open source software before, you're probably familiar with the GitHub slogan: "Build better software, together." Hopefully this book can help you to promote a new idea: "Build connected systems, together."

Who This Book Is For

This book is primarily written for those who want to connect embedded devices to the Internet using Node.js, particularly engineers and designers who want to simplify configuration or monitoring of a device. For reasons we will discuss later, JavaScript is the language of choice in this book. But a number of ideas would also apply to other programming languages (e.g., Ruby, Python, or Arduino's C++).

This book is limited to basic electronics. If you want to go beyond simple outputs such as the "blinking LED" or simple sensors for inputs, you will need to check out other books on embedded systems after reading this one (we'll provide pointers on where to go next).

Finally, this book assumes some basic experience with JavaScript. It is OK if you didn't enjoy JavaScript in the past, and maybe preferred working with Ruby, C, or Python. Hopefully, this book can help you to reconsider that viewpoint and make you want to experiment with JavaScript to build new kinds of connected devices.

How to Use This Book

This book is organized into the following chapters:

Chapter 1, Connecting Worlds
> Here we'll explore JavaScript's role in connecting devices. After a general overview, this chapter delves into more technical details. For those new to JavaScript or Node.js, this chapter will provide some basic information about npm, Node.js modules, buffers, and streams.

Chapter 2, Blink with Arduino
> An LED that blinks is part of many embedded systems. It is also the "Hello, World!" of hardware. Using an Arduino as an example, we'll look deeper into the functional building blocks of a microcontroller and how they can be controlled with JavaScript from the outside.

Chapter 3, Espruino
> This chapter discusses Espruino, which lets you program a microcontroller directly with JavaScript without the need for a host computer. Espruino provides a very lean JavaScript parser that only requires a couple of kilobytes of RAM and flash memory.

Chapter 4, The Tessel 2

Next, we'll review how to get started with Tessel 2, a development platform for prototyping Internet of Things devices.

Chapter 5, Particle Photon

In this chapter, we'll investigate JavaScript toolchains for connecting a microcontroller to the Internet. Our discussion will focus on the Particle Photon.

Chapter 6, Single-Board Computers

The Raspberry Pi is a popular choice for media-related use cases. This chapter looks at different approaches to running Node.js on single-board computers. Various boards will be covered, including the Intel Edison.

Chapter 7, Components for Prototyping

This chapter discusses simple electronic circuits. As outputs, LEDs often indicate the state of a system. For inputs, different components, such as buttons and potentiometers, are usually required. Sensors can capture physical data, and you'll learn some basics about them in this chapter.

Chapter 8, Node.js Libraries for Hardware

Now that you have a strong foundation in boards and components, we'll move on to look closer at working with Node.js libraries for embedded devices. This chapter explores some of the abstractions for hardware. Good examples for talking to hardware with JavaScript can be found in the Johnny-Five library or serialport library for serial communication with Node.js.

Chapter 9, Exploring Network Protocols

Node.js comes with support for a number of different network protocols. After an overview of the Hypertext Transfer Protocol (HTTP), other network protocols are presented. The WebSocket protocol, which is used to push messages over a network, is particularly interesting.

Chapter 10, Web Frontends for Things

Many hardware projects require a user interface (UI). With JavaScript, you can easily build a UI in a web browser. For this, you'll set up a project structure to work with a static HTML page. Then we'll add some JavaScript and SVG for graphics.

Chapter 11, Entering the Cloud

This chapter takes a closer look at sending data with message brokers and MQTT. With MQTT, you can subscribe to updates from sensor devices. In addition, you get an overview of other cloud services for working with messages from devices.

Chapter 12, Making Robots with Node.js

Here we'll cover some basics for building robots with JavaScript. We'll also discuss different approaches for moving a robot using JavaScript.

Chapter 13, Wireless Data with Bluetooth

Bluetooth wireless communication is an important building block to remotely control devices. Some JavaScript libraries for Bluetooth Low Energy will be discussed.

Chapter 14, Toward the Physical Internet

This chapter includes general information about building physical experiences and the role of JavaScript. Instead of delving into technical aspects, the chapter provides a general picture of building digital interfaces in an analog world.

Chapter 15, From Products to Toolkits

As a summary, this chapter takes a broader look at the role of Node.js and embedded devices. Developing modular hardware and software is the main topic of this chapter. You will also learn more about open source hardware.

Conventions Used in This Book

The following typographical conventions are used in this book:

Italic

Indicates new terms, URLs, email addresses, filenames, and file extensions.

`Constant width`

Used for program listings, as well as within paragraphs to refer to program elements such as variable or function names, databases, data types, environment variables, statements, and keywords.

`Constant width bold`

Shows commands or other text that should be typed literally by the user.

`Constant width italic`

Shows text that should be replaced with user-supplied values or by values determined by context.

 This element signifies a tip or suggestion.

This element signifies a general note.

 This element indicates a warning or caution.

Using Code Examples

Supplemental material (code examples, exercises, etc.) is available for download at *https://github.com/embeddednodejs*. Also, you can join the book community online by submitting issues at the book website. Additional resources for the book are published at *http://embeddednodejs.com*.

This book is here to help you get your job done. In general, if example code is offered with this book, you may use it in your programs and documentation. You do not need to contact us for permission unless you're reproducing a significant portion of the code. For example, writing a program that uses several chunks of code from this book does not require permission. Selling or distributing a CD-ROM of examples from O'Reilly books does require permission. Answering a question by citing this book and quoting example code does not require permission. Incorporating a significant amount of example code from this book into your product's documentation does require permission.

We appreciate, but do not require, attribution. An attribution usually includes the title, author, publisher, and ISBN. For example: "*Node.js for Embedded Systems* by Patrick Mulder and Kelsey Breseman (O'Reilly). Copyright 2016 Patrick Mulder and Kelsey Breseman, 978-1-491-92899-8."

If you feel your use of code examples falls outside fair use or the permission given above, feel free to contact us at *permissions@oreilly.com*.

Safari® Books Online

 *Safari Books Online* is an on-demand digital library that delivers expert content in both book and video form from the world's leading authors in technology and business.

Technology professionals, software developers, web designers, and business and creative professionals use Safari Books Online as their primary resource for research, problem solving, learning, and certification training.

Safari Books Online offers a range of plans and pricing for enterprise, government, education, and individuals.

Members have access to thousands of books, training videos, and prepublication manuscripts in one fully searchable database from publishers like O'Reilly Media, Prentice Hall Professional, Addison-Wesley Professional, Microsoft Press, Sams, Que, Peachpit Press, Focal Press, Cisco Press, John Wiley & Sons, Syngress, Morgan Kaufmann, IBM Redbooks, Packt, Adobe Press, FT Press, Apress, Manning, New Riders, McGraw-Hill, Jones & Bartlett, Course Technology, and hundreds more. For more information about Safari Books Online, please visit us online.

How to Contact Us

Please address comments and questions concerning this book to the publisher:

O'Reilly Media, Inc.
1005 Gravenstein Highway North
Sebastopol, CA 95472
800-998-9938 (in the United States or Canada)
707-829-0515 (international or local)
707-829-0104 (fax)

We have a web page for this book, where we list errata, examples, and any additional information. You can access this page at *http://bit.ly/node-js-for-embedded-systems*.

To comment or ask technical questions about this book, send email to *bookquestions@oreilly.com*.

For more information about our books, courses, conferences, and news, see our website at *http://www.oreilly.com*.

Find us on Facebook: *http://facebook.com/oreilly*

Follow us on Twitter: *http://twitter.com/oreillymedia*

Watch us on YouTube: *http://www.youtube.com/oreillymedia*

Acknowledgments

From Patrick

The first ideas for this book resulted from conversations with Denise Jacobs. While I enjoyed working on my first book on building web applications with full-stack JavaScript, I unexpectedly was working with electronics and hardware again. Thanks to Denise, I could find common ground from both worlds. Also, thanks to Denise for submitting that O'Reilly SolidCon talk proposal!

SolidCon was helpful for this book in many ways. Thanks to Jon Bruner for organizing the conference and setting the frame for this book at O'Reilly. SolidCon provided a fantastic platform to discuss how machines can be built, printed, assembled, and programmed. On a philosophical note, SolidCon gave me new ideas for how hardware evolves into a medium for digital expression.

The workshop and discussion with Michael McCool helped me to better structure the material for this book—actually, the current structure of this book is strongly influenced by the workshop Michael gave at SolidCon about the Internet of Things. Also, thanks to Rex St. John, Alexander Tereschenko, and Matthias Hahn for their feedback on early versions of this book.

The book has benefited a lot from discussions I had with Kelsey Breseman from the Tessel project. Thank you, Kelsey, for joining this project as coauthor! Your holistic view on technology improved this book in many ways, and better prepares the reader to tackle the challenges that development of IoT devices pose.

My shift from software to hardware (and back to software) was triggered by a consulting project in Munich. Special thanks to Thorsten Bucksch, who hired me for this project. And thanks to Rainer Brunn, Philip Thurner, Willy Bristiel, and Ralph Mueller-Eschenbach for helpful discussions about electronics.

Many interesting discussions about the Internet of Things happen in makerspaces. Thanks to all friends and meetup members from the Munich Arduino meetup. The mix of learning, teaching, and experimenting shows the power of peer-to-peer networks. In particular, thanks to Thomas Schütt, Augusto Redolfi, Carlos Morras, Rüdiger Freese, Horst Altmann, and Erhard Waretzi for answering "stupid" questions. While I studied electronics many years ago, a lot of its fun came back with exploring Arduino projects. Thanks to Massimo Banzi and his team for building Arduino. And thanks to Dan Hienzsch for building the I2C Education shield.

As the JavaScript community for embedded systems is just evolving, thanks to Rick Waldron for the work on many Node.js libraries that simplify working with embedded systems. Thanks to Ron Evans and Adrian Zankich for presenting Cylon.js at

ScottlandJS in 2014. Thanks to James Halliday for publishing fantastic Node.js modules and for providing early feedback on this book's draft.

Thanks to Jonathan Carter for contributing a discussion about the usage of the Node-Red library.

Without a doubt, this book could not have been written without an "invisible hand." In this case, I want to thank Nan Barber. Writing is hard to plan. Writing is also slow at times, and it's easy to get lost in details. Thanks to Nan for helping to keep us on track. Also thanks to Jasmine, Colleen, and the O'Reilly production team for turning the book draft into a finished book.

For the technical review and feedback on the draft of this book, I want to thank Kevin Sidwar, Rick Waldron, Guido Burger, Gordon Williams, Sandeep Mistry, and Kelsey Breseman.

Last, but not least, I want to thank Béatrice for her love, design inspirations, and support in my writing ambitions.

From Kelsey

My acknowledgments are short because I joined the book quite late in its creation. Primarily, I want to thank Patrick for inviting me into this adventure. It has been a delight to pass ideas and musings back and forth about Node, hardware, and where the Internet might be going.

Thanks also to Jon McKay for always reading over my shoulder, fielding my technical fact-check questions, and generally being supportive.

## CHAPTER 1

Connecting Worlds

JavaScript is unique in its flexibility to run in different environments. Though the language originated in web browsers, JavaScript today drives web applications, and runs in databases and robots, too. In the latter cases, people often use the terms JavaScript and Node.js (a JavaScript runtime environment) interchangeably.

Without JavaScript, connecting devices to networks would entail writing software in three different languages. Embedded devices in particular often require C or C++, while user interfaces in web browsers require web technologies. Besides embedded devices and user interfaces, writing middleware for communication within networks might require yet another programming language.

When working in different environments, JavaScript is an interesting choice—it's becoming *the* universal programming language. This chapter begins with an overview of embedded devices and connecting everything, followed by an introduction to basic JavaScript and its different runtime environments. You will also learn about the background of Node.js.

Why the Internet of Things?

On a physical level, computers are pieces of silicon with hundreds of millions (up to billions) of transistors. The transistors act as switches, either to store state or to run binary operations. In contrast to mechanical switches, transistors act on voltages and electrical signals.

Transistors are getting smaller and smaller. People refer to this phenomenon as *Moore's law*. To understand how it works and where we are going, let's look at computers under a microscope.

Transistors are made from different layers of conducting, isolating, and semi-conducting materials. All layers are added on top of a silicon substrate. The electrical properties of the substrate get altered to form transistors. On top of the transistors, there is a metal layer that allows for the formation of circuits. Figure 1-1 provides a visual explanation of layers on a silicon wafer.

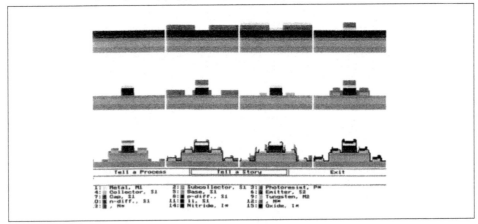

Figure 1-1. Transistors are built by combining layers of isolating, semiconducting, and conducting materials (Drawing by A. C. Redolfi)

The shape of transistors is defined with the help of photolithography. So-called "wafer steppers" project images of transistors on a silicon wafer. These machines are one of the main driving forces behind Moore's law.

By using decreasing wavelengths of light, it was possible to shrink transistors from micrometers in size to tens of nanometers. (It is generally believed that transistors can be shrunk to subnanometer size.)

The increased miniaturization of electronics has resulted in an unprecedented quantity of computing devices in homes, workplaces, and public spaces. It has revolutionized the way we live, travel, learn, and work.

However, until now, most devices have had few ways to directly talk to each other. The idea of an *Internet of Things*, or IoT, predicts that this will change dramatically in the near future, and again revolutionize modern daily life. By connecting devices, engineers are able to create smarter environments for logistics, manufacturing, and healthcare.

Connecting devices requires engineers to solve problems within hardware, software, and network protocols. Let's look closer at embedded devices and how they communicate.

The History of Transistors and Integrated Circuits

In 1947, William Shockley—together with John Bardeen and Walter Brattain—discovered how to build electronic switches from semiconductors.

Then, in 1953, the first computer from transistors was soldered at the University of Manchester. A couple of years later, in 1958, another breakthrough technology was developed by Jack Kilby: the first integrated circuit.

From then on, integration of transistors resulted in all kinds of computing machines, first in rooms and on tables. Later, integrated circuits became part of digital controllers in toys and factories.

The increasing transistor density on chips led Gordon Moore in 1965 to make an important prediction, known as *Moore's law*: he observed that the density of transistors in an integrated circuit doubles every 18 months. Driven by ever-shrinking transistors, the truth (thus far) of Moore's law made calculators and computers affordable to many thousands of companies and millions of users. Despite the doubts of many, Moore's law still holds today.

Embedded Devices

Embedded devices can have many functions. For example, they can play music, track body motion, or identify a parcel in a truck. They often make use of one or more of the building blocks shown in Figure 1-2.

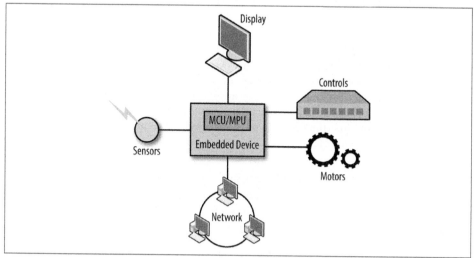

Figure 1-2. Embedded devices consist of many different building blocks

In many cases, their core is a microcontroller unit (MCU) or microprocessor unit (MPU) that is connected to some sensors or a control panel.

Embedded devices monitor an environment or perform autonomous tasks. For monitoring, they need *sensors*. When acting on the physical environment (e.g., with a motor), they require *actuators*.

In contrast to most computers, some embedded devices operate "headless" (i.e., without a graphic display). A fire alarm, for example, has no need for a display, but might need to communicate with a network.

Many embedded devices have power constraints and limited memory for doing computations. This is why programming for embedded devices often is done with lower-level programming languages and often feels difficult.

Some of the frustrations of embedded development can be avoided by using a high-level language such as JavaScript. Previously, memory constraints (among other concerns) made JavaScript a poor choice for embedded devices. But as you will see in this book, JavaScript is becoming an interesting tool for connecting devices to the Internet.

Embedded Internet

The main difference between a "normal" embedded device and an embedded device for IoT is *connectivity.*

By adding links between devices, consumers and companies get new possibilities to track health, coordinate activities, monitor logistics, or improve shopping experiences.

 There has been a recent buzz around connected devices and the IoT. It is often overlooked that devices with network support have been evolving for a number of years. Due to Moore's law and demand for connected hardware like smartphones (driving down component costs), connecting a great number of devices is viable for the first time outside of special realms like medical devices or space vehicles.

Working with remote devices and devices in networks is different from working with a single device. To better capture problems and differences in "systems" of connected devices, experts have created a reference model for the IoT. A simplified version with four abstraction layers is shown in Figure 1-3.

Imagine a new kind of device that plays music but also goes beyond. On the lowest abstraction level, this music player might have sensors that track your activity, motion, and (let's say) the weather. On this "edge" level, it is all about capturing data from sensors.

Abstraction Layer	Technology	Examples
Data Accumulation, "Cloud" Computing	Databases, web browsers, dashboards	Web analytics, web shops, music streaming services, etc.
Edge (Fog) Computing	Semantics, monitoring, transformation	Laptops, smartphones, tablets, etc.
Connectivity	Protocols, routing, security	WiFi, Ethernet, Bluetooth, etc.
Physical Devices & Controllers	Microcontrollers, electronics, AD/DA "raw" data	Sensors, actuators such as loudspeakers and microcontrollers

Figure 1-3. Practical examples of the abstraction layer depicted in the "Internet of Things Reference Model" (http://cdn.iotwf.com/resources/72/IoT_Refer ence_Model_04_June_2014.pdf)

At the next level, the transport of data is essential—for example, to report progress after a workout. But gateways in a network could also help to synchronize your preferences for music when you enter a sports club or download music after a music concert.

On top of that level, some processing happens to filter data for certain events. Typically, a microcontroller or microprocessor could process events and trigger changes in a display or request new information from other places in a network.

Finally, at the highest level, no hardware can be found anymore. Here, the main goals are about analyzing and storing data. This typically involves working with databases, data centers, and monitoring approaches.

Protocols

Links and networks are essential in developing applications for the IoT, so let's explore this road a bit further. The Internet is mostly based on very high-level specifications and protocols. Agreeing to these standards makes interoperation between networks possible.

Figure 1-4 provides a simple diagram of the primary elements of computer networks and how they're interconnected. On an abstract level, computer networks consist of nodes and links. Nodes can be anything from servers, to laptops, to an embedded device. Links can be anything from cables up to wireless connections.

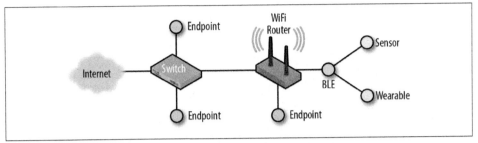

Figure 1-4. Simplified view of a computer network

As programmers, we are often interested in how devices and users talk in a network. When signals hop from node to node, they follow certain rules or *protocols*.

Protocols are built on multiple layers. On the top of the stack, there are application-level protocols:

Hypertext Transfer Protocol (HTTP)
> HTTP was first created to make the transfer of documents across computers easier. It then evolved into a more general protocol to transfer state between devices.

The WebSocket protocol
> Websockets can provide a communication channel between devices. The important advantage of websockets over HTTP is that you can keep a connection open for real time communication.

Besides choices in a protocol stack, the way in which links connect—or connectivity—is important in system design. For many systems, it is important to understand the physical constraints of cables or over-the-air connections. Here are a few types of connections:

Ethernet
> Going back to the origins of computer networks, Ethernet cables played an important role in connecting computers. Ethernet generally provides stable and secure links between devices, compared to wireless connections. However, the disadvantage of using a cable is that it is often inconvenient and sometimes impossible to route to where you need it.

WiFi
> In contrast to Ethernet, wireless networking, or WiFi, provides much more flexibility. Wireless connections have steadily been making progress over the last decade. The login and password for a secured WiFi connection can sometimes be a challenge for getting embedded devices online. Also, data rates can suffer or be limited to smaller spaces depending on the environment of a WiFi router.

USB and serial communication

In embedded development, the Universal Serial Bus (USB) provides a convenient, wired solution for data transfer between the host and an embedded device. Generally, USB is known for its plug-and-play experience. Similar to Ethernet, USB provides a stable and secure link, and can easily transport power to devices. In practice, USB is typically used to connect peripheral devices.

Bluetooth and BLE

In some cases, you only need a wireless connection with a range of a few meters (e.g., if you want to control a light switch from your smartphone). Bluetooth provides peer-to-peer connections. The original Bluetooth protocol had high power consumption, so a new standard—Bluetooth Low Energy (BLE)—was created. Both the original Bluetooth and BLE protocols are in use today, but BLE is more common for IoT applications.

We'll look at more protocols and ways to connect devices throughout this book. Right now it is important to remember that dealing with the IoT requires us to think about many types of abstractions: networks, nodes, links, devices, signals, *and* software. As a result, you need to design "systems" rather than build a single device, server, or process.

To develop a system, you must consider its subsystems and their parts. You need to ask how these connect. This requires you to work with multiple environments at once. One of this book's goals is to show how this can be done with JavaScript.

Examples and Use Cases

Before going into technology details, let's briefly review some common applications for connecting devices. Many technologies are currently just emerging.

One of the visionaries for moving computers into the background of our lives was Mark Weiser (1952–1999), director of the legendary Xerox PARC research laboratory. As he wrote in the *Scientific American* article "The Computer for the 21st Century" in 1991:

Ubiquitous computing names the third wave in computing, just now beginning. First were mainframes, each shared by lots of people. Now we are in the personal computing era, person and machine staring uneasily at each other across the desktop. Next comes ubiquitous computing, or the age of *calm technology*, when technology recedes into the background of our lives.

With decreasing costs of hardware and new software technologies, we'll be able to transform everyday objects into input devices, monitors, or displays. Consider the dining room shown in Figure 1-5, for example.

Figure 1-5. Imagine a dining room with connected devices (photo by Mickey Destr (https://flic.kr/p/9zLbLm))

If you were to start conversations with windows, chairs, tables, or lighting, what would you ask them to do? How would you tell them to behave in the mornings? How about when you have dinner with friends?

Besides having a direct impact on the physical experience of a space, microcontrollers that are connected to networks and databases could influence security and health matters from remote places by sensing your motion and activities, identifying falls, or directly changing your environment in response to external factors. We will discuss this further in Chapter 14.

That may sound like science fiction, but there are already racetracks where you can follow the motion of race cars and obtain all kinds of information about their position in the race. In addition, some car manufacturers offer an API that allows car owners to access information related to energy consumption for their vehicles.

Building these systems will require new approaches to software and hardware development. Instead of long cycles where every building block is engineered in isolation, it is often important to build entire working *systems* quickly. You might be programming displays, blinking LEDs, and working with sensors (all in the same system), as shown in Figure 1-6. Oh, and did we mention that you need to deal with different constraints of hardware and software, too?

When working with systems, modularity plays an important role. This concept allows you to abstract components of the system so that you are not overwhelmed by trying to build from all sides at once. The term *modularity* is used in many contexts, from biology to architecture as well as software development. A good example of modularity is Arduino, which we will discuss in Chapter 2. The standard interface of an Arduino Uno allows you to plug and play, for example, different shields. Devices such as Tessel, discussed later, also take modularity to heart with single-purpose swappable sensors. Modularity plays an important role in JavaScript projects too.

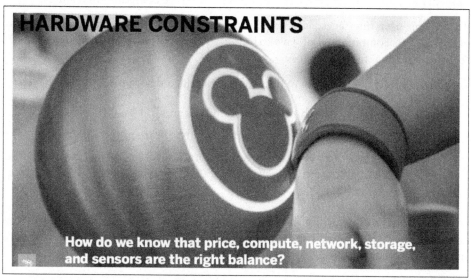

Figure 1-6. A friendship detector with a nontraditional display. Slide taken from a talk by Patrick Kalaher of Frog Design (http://solidcon.com/internet-of-things-2015/public/schedule/detail/40837).

JavaScript for Distributed Programming

By now, you have seen a number of examples on what the IoT means when working with multiple environments at the same time. Because it can be used at so many levels, JavaScript is a promising language to tackle the problems of the IoT.

JavaScript and the IoT

Let's now review what makes JavaScript an interesting choice for IoT development.

First, JavaScript is in wide use. A large number of web developers are familiar with it. While the language began as scripting language for web browsers, its programming model has been widely adapted for other environments too, such as web application servers or mobile web browsers.

In addition, because there is a large programming community behind it, JavaScript is well documented and there is good standardization across different implementations.

From this, a strong ecosystem with many open source libraries comes as an important bonus.

Generally, JavaScript engines are high performance. Applications running on Chrome V8 can be very fast. The power of this trend can be seen by recent efforts to play 3D games in a web browser (*https://www.youtube.com/watch?v=aZqhRICne_M*). Developments such as SIMD.js even expose high-performance computation features.

To develop user interfaces, JavaScript can be used with web technologies such as HTML5. The combination of JavaScript and HTML5 is useful for developing UI "companion apps" for IoT devices.

Last, but not least, JavaScript is well suited to embedded device programming:

- JavaScript supports asynchronous function calls and I/O
- Asynchronous calls are useful for event-driven hardware programming
- Node.js provides hooks to integrate linked libraries from code that is written in C or C++; take a look at *https://nodejs.org/api/addons.html* and *https://github.com/nodejs/nan* for more details

In the next section, we will briefly review some JavaScript basics. We'll also look at running JavaScript in a web browser as well as with Node.js. The sections to come are mainly a refresher for those who are new to JavaScript.

Hello World with JavaScript

First appearing in 1995, JavaScript was initially aimed at "nonprofessional" programmers. When it was first specified, it took constructs from a number of other languages.

Installing nvm

JavaScript originated in web browsers from different companies, so Netscape decided to standardize the language under the name of ECMAScript. A lot has happened since the first JavaScript specification—and the evolution of the language is ongoing. A nice tool to experiment with language improvement is nvm, the Node Version Manager. You can install it from *https://github.com/creationix/nvm*.

Once installed, you can select Node.js versions with:

```
$ nvm install 4.0.0
$ nvm use 4.0.0
```

Many embeddeded devices still run Node.js versions 0.12.4 or even 0.10.x.

Basic syntax

JavaScript is an object-oriented programming language. Its syntax is C-like, but in many cases simpler. Assigning a value to a variable is done as follows:

```
var foo = "Hello World.";
```

With this assignment, you create a variable foo that references the String "Hello World". That variable is declared by adding the var keyword in the beginning.

Statements normally end with a semicolon. The semicolon can be replaced by a comma, if you do multiple assignments as follows:

```
var foo = "Hello",
    bar = " World.";
```

The String objects in the preceding snippet are declared with double quotes. It is also possible to use single quotes to declare strings, which is common in many libraries:

```
var foo = 'Hello World.';
```

Note that JavaScript is dynamically typed. This means that, unlike C or Java, you don't have to define the type of variable before runtime. Some examples:

```
var foo = 1;
var bar = 1.21;
```

Looking at numbers, there are no integer types in JavaScript. All numbers are floats. If you work with large numbers and want to avoid dealing with rounding problems, you can use some of the BigInt libraries in Node.js.

Higher-level functions

Functions are an important class of JavaScript objects. Interestingly, functions can be bound to variables too. This allows us to pass around functions as arguments. For example:

```
var blink = function() {
  console.log('blink');
};
setInterval(blink, 1000);
```

By passing the function blink to another function setInterval, blink is called in 1-second intervals (1,000 milliseconds is equivalent to 1 second).

Functions have a "scope" to resolve the state of their inner code bodies. In older Java-Script versions, scope was only bound to a function, not to a block of code. This has changed in newer versions. Since ECMAScript 2015 (*http://www.ecma-international.org/ecma-262/6.0*), lexical declaration bindings formed with let and const are block scoped.

To understand what this means, consider the following examples:

```
// function scope
var foo = 1;
var bar = function() {
    console.log(foo);
}
bar();
```

Lexical scope allows proper *closures*.

Closures are a concept from functional programming. During evaluation, the runtime first checks the environment of the bar function. When the variable foo is not found inside the function bar, the runtime looks further in the parameter list bindings. If the foo binding is not found in the parameter list bindings, the runtime looks to the outer environment (the lexical environment of a function) and there it finds a foo binding.

Compare this to the behavior of variables that are defined with let or const:

```
// block scope
var outside = 1;
const constNumber = 42;
function printBlock() {
  let inside = 3;
  console.log(outside, inside, constNumber);
}
printBlock();
```

If you play with the variables *inside* and *outside*, you'll see how let and const help to preserve the value from the original scope.

Dealing with scope requires some practice, especially if you are new to JavaScript. Also, scope is generally static, except for this.

With this, you can reference context inside an object, as we will see next.

Objects and arrays

First, objects and associative arrays look the same:

```
// a simple robot object
var robot = {}
robot['hand'] = 'up';
robot.hand = 'up';
```

JavaScript uses the idea of object "prototype" to generate new objects. Object prototypes can be cloned with the new operator as follows:

```
function Robot() {};
var robot = new Robot();
```

Within objects, the `this` variable can be used to refer to the current object:

```
robot.raiseHand = function() {
  this.hand = 'up';
};
```

Depending where you are in your program, the reference to `this` can change. Often, we want to "bind" a `this` context to objects. In that way, we can call functions on objects without worrying about the calling context of a function.

JSON

The JavaScript object literal syntax is a key-value pair:

```
var robot = {
    hand: 'up',
    raiseHand: function() {}
}
```

When you want to transport JavaScript objects from one place to another (such as over an internet connection), JavaScript Object Notation (JSON) syntax for object properties is used:

```
{
    "hand": "up",
    "legs": "down"
}
```

JSON is a serialization-safe subset of JavaScript (i.e., there are no functions and all property names are double-quoted). JSON can be found in all kinds of software systems—in particular, it is increasingly used in web development to replace XML formats.

Reading about code examples gets boring quickly. Let's now look at how to run Java-Script in the web browser and with Node.js.

JavaScript Runtime Environments

JavaScript can run in multiple environments. In this book, there are three environments of interest: web browsers, web application servers, and embedded devices. Let's first look at the web browser, which is where many software developers first encounter JavaScript.

The Browser

JavaScript has its origins in web browsers. If you haven't developed in a web browser before, have a look at the screenshot in Figure 1-7.

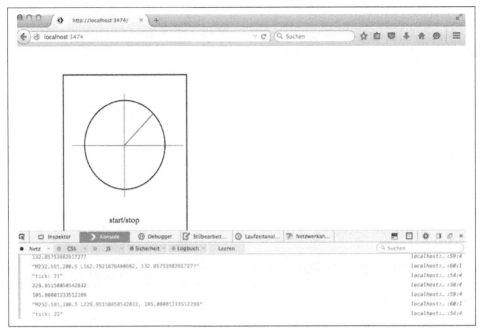

Figure 1-7. Working with JavaScript in a web browser

In most web browsers, you can inspect a web page by right-clicking and selecting the appropriate option. You'll find a developer console where you can try out the Java-Script statements from above. If this is new for you, we recommend you try a few of the exercises found at JavaScript for Cats (*http://jsforcats.com*), a brief workshop for JavaScript in the browser built by Max Ogden.

Web browsers often come with an integrated debugger that allows you to set break-points. This is often a good idea to understand what is going on. We'll look closer at JavaScript in the browser in Chapter 10.

The Server

The foundations of JavaScript on the server were built in 2008 when Google released the open source JavaScript engine V8. The V8 project is part of the Google Chrome web browser.

One year later, Ryan Dahl released Node.js. He added an event loop and low-level JavaScript APIs for the filesystem and drivers for hardware. And, thanks to V8, it can run on the world's most important computing platforms, from servers to tablets and smartphones.

An important part of the Node.js ecosystem is based on npm, the Node Package Manager. Packages can be published to the npm registry, which includes more than 100,000 open source packages that you can download, modify, and use in your programs.

For example, if you needed to find a library to develop with I2C tags,[1] you could search the npm website by typing "i2c" in the search bar, as shown in Figure 1-8.

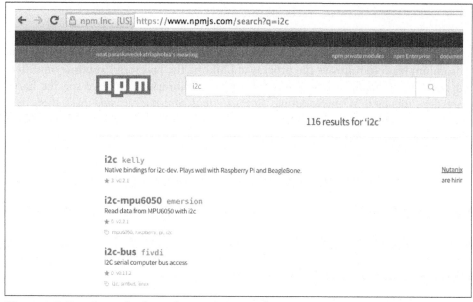

Figure 1-8. Search results from the npmjs.com website

To install the library called "i2c" to your current directory with npm, you would enter into the console:

```
$ npm install i2c
```

This command downloads the library and its dependencies in a directory called *node_modules*.

Besides installing packages, npm can be used to set up a project manifest file with:

```
$ npm init
```

When starting with a fresh project, it is often a good idea to run this command first.

---

1 I2C is a serial communication protocol. See the NXP datasheets (*http://www.nxp.com/documents/user_manual/UM10204.pdf*) for further detail.

Some of the packages from npm can be installed globally as command-line tools. We'll need a number of those tools, such as Browserify. To install a package globally, you would run:

```
$ npm install -g browserify
```

For some libraries, such as the serialport library, during the installation you'll see something like this:

```
> node-pre-gyp install --fallback-to-build
```

The node commands end with gyp, which stands for "generate your projects." The gyp (*https://en.wikipedia.org/wiki/GYP_(software)*) tools were developed by the Chromium team to improve the process of building the JavaScript runtime on different platforms. This approach works for JavaScript libraries that have specific hardware dependencies. With Node-gyp (*https://github.com/nodejs/node-gyp*), there is a wrapper for gyp to compile native C/C++ into a Node library. This allows Node projects to interface with very low-level hardware libraries on different platforms.

You should definitely also check out nan (*https://github.com/nodejs/nan*) (Node Native Addons) if you need to bind code in C or C++ to JavaScript.

Embedded Devices

JavaScript's asynchronous programming model and its large ecosystem also make it interesting for programming embedded devices. There are several options to work with JavaScript inside and outside of an embedded device.

Projects such as Espruino (*https://github.com/espruino/Espruino*), Kinoma.js (*https://github.com/kinoma/kinomajs*), and iotjs (*https://github.com/Samsung/iotjs*) allow you to run a subset of JavaScript directly on a microcontroller. Espruino and Kinoma.js allow you to buy boards on which JavaScript runs natively.

A number of embedded devices support running scripting languages. Because of its compact size, some developers have explored using the Lua language (*https://en.wikipedia.org/wiki/Lua_(programming_language)*) on embedded devices. By combining the advantages of Lua and JavaScript, the Tessel 1 explored the idea of transpiling JavaScript to Lua—for an example, see the Colony-Compiler (*https://github.com/tessel/colony-compiler*).

The newer Tessel 2 combines a microcontroller with a "system-on-chip" (SoC) which includes a microprocessor. This hybrid approach is very promising because it affords low-level interfaces (microcontroller) with high-level abstractions (microprocessor running Linux).

With this strategy, you can run JavaScript on an embedded device by installing the same Node.js runtime that web developers use for web applications or browser programming. All you need is some embedded Linux (as you will see later in the book, embedded Linux is available for a number of boards). This strategy is adopted by boards such as the Intel Edison, BeagleBone, Raspberry Pi, and Tessel 2.

The embedded Linux approach is interesting for a couple of reasons:

- The runtime performance of the JavaScript V8 engine on an embedded device is very good compared to compiled code and to other high-level languages.
- JavaScript libraries and developers can build upon existing know-how for network protocols, filesystems, drivers, and databases. Power and memory can be constraints; however, if you have WiFi, you will draw a fair amount of power regardless of the workload on an application processor.
- As Moore's law continues to make computing resources cheaper, small operating systems with support of JavaScript can directly run on battery-powered devices too. Within the next few years, we will hopefully see innovations to reduce power consumption and improve battery life.

At this stage, the main problem with using JavaScript on an embedded device is the size of the Node.js runtime, which requires a good deal of memory on the device. On a laptop or server, a simple web server can take up to 50 MB of disk space. Many embedded devices have less disk space, and even less RAM to respond to incoming requests.

Luckily, there are projects that aim to reduce the hunger for memory. One such project is JXcore (*http://jxcore.com*), which makes it possible to run Node.js apps on a wide range of devices and platforms. Also, ChaiScript (*http://chaiscript.com*) draws inspiration from the JavaScript syntax to bind powerful C++ code. With this you can add scripting functionalities to C++ code for embedded applications.

Installing JXcore

With JXcore, it should become possible to host a fully functional chat server on a small WiFi router with only 16 MB memory. The current aim is to limit the JavaScript runtime to below 1 MB.

Binaries for JXcore are available for different boards, including the Intel Galileo or Edison (ia32), the RiotBoard (Android ARM), and Raspberry Pi (Debian ARM). You can also run JXcore on Mac OS X or Windows. To use JXcore, you can download the runtime from *http://jxcore.com/downloads*.

Once downloaded, you can add JXcore to the path environment variable of your system. Then you will be able to run jx from the command line similar as you would run node. In contrast to Node.js, JXcore allows you to package an app to run natively on a system. Instructions for how to do this can be found at *http://jxcore.com/turn-node-applications-into-executables*.

The Node.js API

Node.js comes with a number of different modules that are important when looking at hardware. See the Node.js API documentation (*https://nodejs.org/api/documenta tion.html*) for more information. The following sections provide an overview of buffers and streams.

Buffer

You will encounter buffers in many Node.js libraries related to hardware and network protocols. The idea of buffers is to provide some minimal "typing" to an array of bytes.

In computers, there are different ways to group bits into numbers. For example, for serial communication between devices, numbers are collected in memory "buffers." In Node.js, a buffer object can manage memory content and values. But buffers also provide an easy way to convert numbers from a hex format to decimal representation, and vice versa.

A good way to learn about buffers is via the Node.js console. First, you create a new "memory" buffer that has some random values by default. From Node's REPL (entered by typing node into the console), type:

```
> var buf = new Buffer(4);
<Buffer 50 0a 00 03>
```

In the preceding example, you have 4 bytes, or 32 bits, of memory to work with. Buffers are not initialized by default. To fill the buffer with empty values, there is the fill method:

```
> buf.fill(0);
<Buffer 00 00 00 00>
```

Buffers become more interesting when reading or writing values.

To write data, there are several options depending on the size of the buffer. A very useful form of data in a buffer are unsigned integers (uint). 8 bits can represent values from 0x00 to 0xFF which you can see below. With buf.writeUint8, you can write unsigned integers at a position in the buffer:

```
> buf.writeUint8(0x78, 2);
> console.log(buf)
<Buffer 00 00 78 00>
```

To read content from a buffer, you can then use the `readUint8` function as follows:

```
> buf.readUint8(2);
120
```

The value 120 is the decimal representation of the hex value `0x78`. The content of a buffer often represents characters that are human readable. To convert numbers to readable characters, you can apply the `toString()` method:

```
> console.log(buf.toString());
x
```

Note that you would see Unicode characters if you just looked at the return value of `buf.toString()`. Unicode characters are useful in the context of non-Western alphabets or special symbols such as emojis.

In hardware, the `hex` representation is sometimes the most interesting. To see the hex values of a buffer, you can add a `'hex'` argument to `toString()`:

```
> console.log(buf.toString('hex'))
00007800
```

To understand data from an embedded device, you often want to create a buffer with numbers in hex format. A buffer can help in these cases:

```
> var buf2 = new Buffer('deadbeef', 'hex');
> console.log(buf2);
<Buffer de ad be ef>
```

The `buffer` module provides more ways to manage large chunks of binary numbers (e.g., 16-bit values or numbers in big-endian or little-endian notation). For now, remember that buffers allow you to easily speak and explore Hexspeak (*https://en.wikipedia.org/wiki/Hexspeak*). that helps to control digital blocks of embedded devices.

Streams

Node.js is not only known for efficient processing of events from different sources. Its relationship to data via JSON makes Node.js special compared to other programming environments too.

A fundamental concept of working with data and bytes in Node.js are streams. Streams help you to observe and manipulate the flow of data over time. They can be anything that relates to data—for example, raw bytes of music, data strings from a database, or web pages from a web server. Take a look at the documentation of incoming HTTP requests (*https://nodejs.org/api/http.html#http_http_incomingmessage*) to see an important usage of streams.

Besides managing data in networks or databases, streams are nice to deal with user input too. Input from a user can be captured with a writable stream:

```
// import stream libraries
var stream = require('stream');
var Stream = stream.Stream;

// create new stream to capture data
var ws = new Stream();
ws.writable = true;

// define write behavior
ws.write = function(data) {
  console.log("input=" + data);
}

// when closing a stream
ws.end = function(data) {
  console.log("bye");
}

// combine stream from input to output
process.stdin.pipe(ws);
```

A simple test shows how this works:

```
$ node pipe_out.js
hello
input=hello
```

The writable stream handles "write" and "end" events from the standard input. This connection is made by piping standard input to the writable stream. You could also pipe the output of a file into the write stream. For example:

```
$ echo hello | node pipe_out.js
input=hello

bye
```

## CHAPTER 2

Blink with Arduino

When you learn a new programming language, the first exercise is usually to display "Hello, World!" on a screen. When working with a new embedded device, the equivalent first exercise is to blink a light, often an LED. By toggling an LED, you check that the main parts of a system are working and that you can control them. Arduinos are famous for letting users get LEDs to blink very easily. Because it's easy to get up and running with Arduino, you'll be able to quickly get a feel for where and why JavaScript can be used in an embedded system.

To begin, what does it take to toggle an LED on and off? From a hardware perspective, most boards with a microcontroller have LEDs for debugging built in. And from a JavaScript viewpoint, controlling the blink of an LED can be as simple as:

```
led.toggle();
```

However, to run this code, you need to set up the hardware. If you want to control an external LED, you must build a small electronic circuit. Depending on which board you use, you might need to configure a toolchain and connect a special device called a "programmer" to flash the board—JavaScript is the easy part.

Starting with an Arduino is very helpful in exploring the building blocks of a simple embedded device. For this, you must set up the pins of a microcontroller unit and build basic electronic circuits. Understanding the building blocks and their configurations can be challenging.

For this reason, we will begin with a discussion with Arduino. Broadly speaking, an Arduino is a board with a microcontroller. It's not necessary to buy all of the boards we'll cover, but it is important to understand these components on a basic level because the chips on a board define the behavior of the embedded system. Experiences with one chipset might apply to projects with other chips at a later stage.

Getting Started with Microcontrollers

Microcontroller units (MCUs) typically live in watches, pocket calculators, or small radios.

As shown in Figure 2-1, a microcontroller provides *input* and *output* pins to interact with a physical environment. Besides physical pins, a microcontroller can also run small programs to process events from pins with the help of its instruction set.

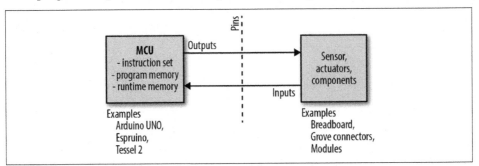

Figure 2-1. Microcontrollers provide pins and programming capabilites

An instruction set of a microcontroller only supports a number of operations, such as basic arithmetic operations or manipulation of the control flow in a program.

Because most programmers find it difficult to write programs with instructions in hex code, programs for a microcontroller are usually compiled from a higher-level language. The resulting binary is stored in the flash memory of the MCU, sometimes refered to as *read-only memory* (ROM). This memory is nonvolatile, meaning after power on and off, the content remains. The size of the flash memory is typically 32 KB for an Arduino.

In contrast, the "static RAM" (SRAM) of a microcontroller stores variables during program execution. The SRAM is volatile—that is, after you power off the device, the content is lost. SRAM is also smaller than flash memory, typically 1–2 KB for an Arduino.

MCUs can only run tiny programs, but because of this trade-off, they consume only a few milliamperes of current (between 10–20 mA for an average Arduino) during operation. This makes MCUs a good fit when building devices that must run on a battery.

As we will discuss later in this chapter, microcontrollers are also interesting because you must capture signals from pins in "real time." For now, it is only important to remember that a microcontroller has more building blocks than a central processing unit (CPU).

If you begin searching around online for microcontroller starter kits, you'll quickly discover a wide variety of products with many different chips. In particular, Arduino, Espruino, and Tessel 2 have succeeded in making microcontrollers accessible to a wide audience. We'll discuss Espruino and Tessel 2 in Chapters 3 and 4, respectively. But first, let's take a look at Arduino.

Arduino

If you want to explore electronics and hardware, one category of boards is especially popular: Arduino boards.

Arduino is a pioneer of open source hardware.[1] This means you can find schematics and board layouts on the Internet to help you configure your own embedded devices. For example, Figure 2-2 shows the board layout of the Arduino Uno.

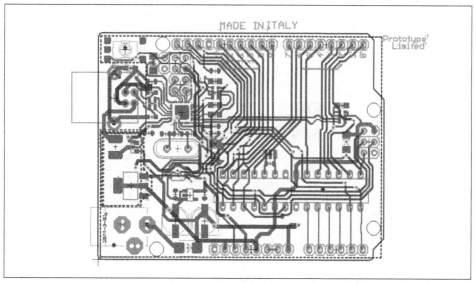

Figure 2-2. Most Arduino boards are open source hardware (source: https://www.ardu ino.cc/en/main/arduinoBoardUno)

Besides the Arduino Uno, there are many other types of Arduino boards, such as Arduino Nano, Leonardo, Micro, and Mega. Most Arduino boards have an ATmega328 microcontroller from Atmel. The ATmega328 has an 8-bit instruction set, 32 KB of flash memory, and 1–2 KB of RAM. Compared to most modern computers, this is not much.

---

1 We will further discuss the importance of open source hardware in Chapter 14.

If you find these numbers confusing, you can get an idea of the performance differences through the following metaphor: a microcontroller is like a small animal—a swift cat, for example. Compare this cat to an elephant, which can carry a lot of weight, but needs many more resources to survive. Your computer (a processor) is an elephant compared to a microcontroller. Both animals have useful features.

While you can buy Arduino boards for around $20, you can also find Arduino clones from China for a couple bucks. With cheap boards, you will sometimes need workarounds such as special drivers for the serial port.

An example of an Arduino is shown in Figure 2-3. The board is connected to a Grove header shield and a push button. Grove headers and connectors are the white connectors to mount components (as will be discussed in Chapter 7). The Arduino Nano is a nice board to have, because besides being cheap, it has a very small form factor (hence its name).

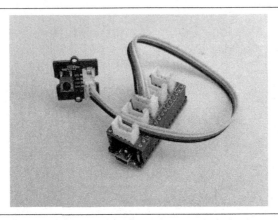

Figure 2-3. Arduino Nano with Grove headers and push button

You'll need to consider the purpose and scope of your project before deciding which Arduino boards to work with—each board has special features that you'll want to consider as you explore electronics and hardware. Note that the form factor of an Arduino Uno board has become very popular. Peripheral devices and circuits can be directly plugged into the board with Arduino-compatible shields, which makes Arduino *modular*. Similar to combining code libraries, you can reuse the hardware shields on top of an Arduino.

Besides a board, you'll need some components to work with. For example, Figure 2-3 shows an Arduino Nano with a push button. This example uses a "shield" with Grove headers where you can connect components. Shields and components will be discussed in Chapter 7.

Because most Arduinos only have 32 KB of flash memory, the space for a JavaScript runtime environment is rather limited. Memory in general puts hard constraints on efficiency and code size on a microcontroller. For this reason, many programmers choose a hybrid approach of using JavaScript outside of and C inside of an embedded device.

The Arduino IDE removes a lot of obstacles that make embedded development hard. But beware: many programmers will advise you to learn C and C++ at some point. In comparison to JavaScript, C programming offers more control over a machine. However, it takes time to learn about the compilers, linkers, and operating systems that go along with C programming. We advise you to use JavaScript first. If you then want to go beyond programming embedded systems with JavaScript, *Making Embedded Systems* by Elecia White (O'Reilly, 2011) is a good start.

The Blink Sketch

To blink an LED, you have to run a "sketch" on the Arduino. An Arduino sketch hides a lot of the complexity from a microcontroller. The Arduino IDE comes with a number of sketch examples to learn embedded development. Writing, building, and uploading a Blink sketch will give you a first feeling of how microcontrollers work.

Installing the Arduino IDE

The Arduino IDE can be downloaded from *https://www.arduino.cc/en/Main/Soft ware*. The latest version at the time of this writing is 1.6.12. The Arduino IDE is based on a Java Virtual Machine, and runs on Windows, Mac OS X, and Linux.

Once the package is downloaded and installed, you'll be able to use the IDE with different Arduino boards. Depending on the board manufacturer, you may need to install some additional drivers to program a board, such as drivers from FTDI (*http://www.ftdichip.com/Drivers/VCP.htm*). As a rule of thumb, the cheaper a board, the harder it might be to find the right drivers.

During installation of the IDE, you might want to take a look at the Arduino Language Reference (*http://arduino.cc/en/Reference/HomePage*) to find out more about the programming constructs. Also, there is a vast number of open source libraries that solve many existing problems. Arduino supports multiple hardware boards from very small microcontrollers up to powerful microprocessor boards.

If you create a new Arduino sketch, you'll see the following basic code structure:

```
void setup() {
}

void loop() {
}
```

These two functions are the foundation of every Arduino program. The setup() function is where you put code to configure the hardware and initialize variables. This function will only run once when your Arduino is turned on. The loop() function is where the the "main" program goes. We'll see shortly how this looks for a blinking LED. Note that most Arduino boards have an LED connected to pin 13, which you can easily toggle for testing.

The separation of code into setup() and main loop() is common in the embedded world. First, you'll have a function to configure your microcontroller and peripherals. Then follows an infinite loop, where different instructions are executed. The code in the infinite loop is repeated as long as the device has power. To make an LED blink with an Arduino forever, you would use the following:

```
void setup() {
    // initialize the digital pin as an output.
    pinMode(13, OUTPUT);
}

void loop() {
    digitalWrite(13, HIGH);   // turn LED on
    delay(1000);              // wait for a second
    digitalWrite(13, LOW);    // toggle LED
    delay(400);               // wait 400 ms
}
```

While keywords such as void are part of C, Arduino programs contain more keyword-like commands such as pinMode, delay, and digitalWrite as just shown. These commands are part of a *hardware abstraction layer* (or HAL) Arduino provides to hide the lower-level complexities of a microcontroller. No matter which Arduino board you use, these statements are properly translated to pin configurations. By the way, pinMode configures the mode of a pin (i.e., if it is an input or output). If a pin is configured as output, you can write state with digitalWrite. If the pin is an input, you can read state with digitalRead.

Note the name of the instructions to change the state of pins. The Arduino nomenclature has made its way into some JavaScript libraries, as you will see shortly. Before examining how, let's see the Arduino example in action.

A look at the Arduino IDE (shown in Figure 2-4) quickly reveals two functions: a "verify" button that *compiles* C and C++ to byte sequences that a microcontroller can run and an "upload" button that places your code in the free program memory of a microcontroller (ROM).

Figure 2-4. The Arduino IDE

If you have an Arduino and press the compile button, in the console you will see:

```
Sketch uses 1,030 bytes (3%) of program storage space. Maximum is 30,720 bytes.
Global variables use 9 bytes (0%) of dynamic memory, leaving 2,039 bytes for
    local variables. Maximum is 2,048 bytes.
```

This shows how compact the code is. The code will use only 1 KB of flash memory. And, only 9 bytes of RAM are necessary!

Next, you can press the upload button. After a brief wait while the device is flashed, you will see LED 13 blinking, as shown in Figure 2-5.

Figure 2-5. The default LED to blink on the Arduino Uno

Similarly, you could explore using input pins or different forms of output signals. We'll discuss more features of microcontrollers later. Let's first look at controlling an Arduino with JavaScript.

The Firmata Bridge

While Arduino sketches (or more specifically, custom firmware development) give you compact code, it can be easier to share, explore, and manage libraries for embedded devices with JavaScript.

To use an Arduino with JavaScript (and Ruby, Python, and other scripting languages), Arduino provides standard firmware that makes pins accessible via serial communication. Basically, Firmata turns a microcontroller into a "client" that follows commands from a "host" computer.

Firmata is an open protocol similar to the MIDI protocol used to compose music for different devices. Like the MIDI protocol, the Firmata protocol can be used to talk with many different embedded devices.

Arduino provides Firmata as a sketch. You can flash Firmata within the Arduino IDE to an Arduino by navigating to Examples → Firmata → StandardFirmata. Once you have the Firmata code running on the Arduino, you can start using all kinds of client software on your host computer.

Flashing Firmata from the Command Line

There are a number of Node.js utilities that provide flashing support for Firmata from the command line. With that approach, you can flash an Arduino without loading the Arduino IDE.

One Node.js tool is firmata-party (*https://www.npmjs.com/package/firmata-party*). To install this tool, you write:

```
$ npm install -g firmata-party
```

If you then attach an Arduino Uno via USB to your laptop, you can download Firmata to the Arduino with the following command:

```
$ firmata-party uno --debug
found uno on port /dev/cu.usbmodem14131
connected
reset complete.
flashing, please wait...
flash complete.
```

From now on, you can easily interact with the Arduino via Firmata. Other flashing tools are Nodebots-Interchange (*https://github.com/j5js/nodebots-interchange*) and avrgirl-arduino (*https://github.com/noopkat/avrgirl-arduino*).

To test that flashing Firmata was successful, you have several options. First, on the Firmata website, you will find a number of Firmata clients (*http://www.firmata.org/wiki/Download*). The Firmata Test Program (*http://www.firmata.org/wiki/Main_Page#Firmata_Test_Program*) is a popular debugging tool. Figure 2-6 shows the UI.

Second, you can interact with Firmata from a web browser with browser plugins. If you want to try, you can download the Google Chrome Firmata plugin. It will give you a similar user interface as the standalone Firmata test application.

The Firmata protocol is also a popular choice to get started with Node.js and embedded systems. By using Firmata, you can do a lot of computing on a host computer. The control of a microcontroller from outside is also the disadvantage of using Firmata: you'll need to have a host computer connected to your microcontroller in order to have it doing something useful.

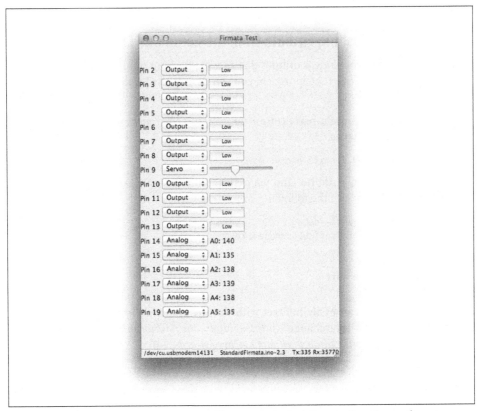

Figure 2-6. The Firmata test program offers a way to test the pin functions of a micro-controller

Programming an Arduino with JavaScript

Once you have checked your connection to an Arduino with a Firmata test client, you can bind a JavaScript process to your board.

To talk with Firmata from JavaScript, you can use the Firmata library, originally written by Julian Gautier and currently maintained by Rick Waldron.

In a new project, you can start with:

```
$ npm init --y
$ npm install --save firmata
```

With this library, we can connect to input and output pins.

Let's look at a blinking LED again:

```
// blink_led.js
// the Firmata protocol provides a simple protocol to an embedded system
var Board = require('firmata');
```

```
Board.requestPort(function(error, port) {
  if (error) {
    console.log(error);
    return;
  }
  var board = new Board(port.comName);

  // start to blink when the Arduino is ready
  board.on("ready", function() {

    // main part
    console.log('connected:  ' +  modem);
    var ledOn = true;

    // configure pin 13 as output
    board.pinMode(13, board.MODES.OUTPUT);
    // blink the LED
    setInterval(function() {
      if (ledOn) {
        console.log('ON');
        board.digitalWrite(13, board.HIGH);
      } else {
        console.log('OFF');
        board.digitalWrite(13, board.LOW);
      }
      ledOn = !ledOn;
    }, 500);
  });
});
```

To blink the LED, run the preceding script with Node.js:

```
$ node blink_led
```

If everything worked, you should see the LED turning on and off. This is also a good moment to compare the differences in code expressed in terms of Arduino and Java-Script.

In the JavaScript example, you get a board object, where you can listen to *events* from the hardware. For the blink example, you first wait until the board emits the "ready" event (the connection works properly). Once this happens, you can change the state of the board with functions using digitalWrite and pinMode. You could easily inter-act with the JavaScript board object in a web server or web interface too (we'll discuss how to do this in Chapters 9 and 10).

Functional Blocks of an MCU

Now that we've looked at some examples of how to blink an LED, think about this for a second: the LED is connected to a *pin* of a microcontroller. The pin acts as the inter-face from the program code to some concrete electrical signal. Pins can be grouped by functional blocks—for example, inputs or outputs or pins for communication. Inside a microcontroller, pins can be attached to *timers* to work with signals in real time. Understanding the role of pins can be difficult; to aid your understanding, it's often beneficial to consult pinout diagrams (which we'll discuss later in this section).

Pins

Pins of an MCU come in two categories: *inputs* and *outputs*. A pin can either "drive" signals to peripherals and components, or it can "detect" changes from the outside.

Inputs and outputs are technically quite different. While inputs are all about capturing the state of signals, outputs can drive current into components. Because Arduino boards are capable of driving several milliamperes of current, they're a good fit for controlling small actuators such as motors or lights.

Besides acting as "force" (output pin) or "sink" (input pin), pins carry *analog* or *digital* signal types (see the following sidebar for details on how this works).

Digital Versus Analog Signals

As shown in Figure 2-7, there are two fundamentally different kinds of signals in embedded devices: digital and analog. Digital signals carry information based on "discrete" states. For binary, digital signals, a low voltage corresponds to a logical LOW state. A high voltage corresponds to a logical HIGH state. The voltage ranges that are read as "high" or "low" depend on the microcontroller and will be specified in its datasheet. The bits that are encoded in a digital signal can transmit data or commands. Digital signals are typically very robust to noise.

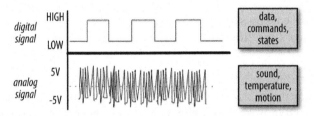

Figure 2-7. Digital versus analog signals

On the other hand, an analog signal can take an infinite range of states. The output of a sensor usually comes as an analog signal. Analog signals are also important for generating outputs such as sounds in a loudspeaker. You can make analog signals visible with the help of an oscilloscope. Analog signals can easily be corrupted by noise from their electrical environment.

When writing embedded software, the first step is to locate and configure the pins of the microcontroller. For example, an Arduino Uno has 5 analog inputs and 13 digital pins known as general-purpose input/outputs (GPIOs). Of these 13 GPIOs, 5 pins can emulate an analog output with the help of pulse-width modulation (PWM), as will be discussed in "Pulse-Width Modulation" on page 39.

On an Arduino, you first configure the direction of a pin. To *read* data from it with software, you must configure the pin as *input*. With Arduino and Firmata, if you want GPIO pin 12 to be an input, you would configure it as follows:

```
board.pinMode(12, board.MODES.INPUT);
```

Or, to *write* data to another device, you can configure another pin as *output*:

```
board.pinMode(12, board.MODES.OUTPUT);
```

On an Arduino, toggling a digital pin to a high voltage is done with:

```
board.digitalWrite(13, board.HIGH);
```

To write a low voltage, you would write:

```
board.digitalWrite(13, board.LOW);
```

Besides simple inputs and outputs, port pins often provide more functions. This means you not only can read a digital state, or write it, you can also start up special forms of communication, such as PWM and hardware communication protocols.

When different resources on a chip use the same port pins, we are referring to "multiplexing" pin functions. The way this works is defined by the chip architecture of a microcontroller defines how multiplexing works. Let's dig into the building blocks of a microcontroller starting with its CPU.

Microcontroller Versus Microprocessor

On top of providing pins for building circuits, microcontrollers can run programs with the help of a CPU. The datasheets for a microcontroller provide all the details, and the following specs are of particular interest:

- The amount of memory (volatile and nonvolatile) to store variables and code
- The type of instruction set to execute code and operations with variables
- The timers to change pin states with high timing accuracy
- The power consumption at a certain operating frequency

Compared to the CPU of a bigger computer, these parameters make a microcontroller nice for embedded systems on a battery. Moreover, the costs of microcontrollers can be significantly lower than those of microprocessors (though microprocessors are becoming cheaper due to high volume demands).

However, microcontrollers also have disadvantages. In particular, their performance for computations can be a problem. If you want to connect a microcontroller to a network, or if you want to run a web server or database, this is where *microprocessors* become very interesting.

Microprocessors (MPUs) have many more pins, more memory, and much more power for computations. The boundaries between MCU and MPU are not always clear, but you will usually have to deal with some tradeoffs when chosing a board with a microcontroller or microprocessor.

 The choice between MCU or MPU can be difficult. Many suppliers provide white papers to make it easier to understand what your application requires. For example, Atmel's paper "Microprocessor (MPU) or Microcontroller (MCU)?" (*http://www.atmel.com/ images/mcu_vs_mpu_article.pdf*) provides some additional insight.

In earlier code examples, we worked with a number of functional blocks of a microcontroller. As you can see from the block diagram, Arduino provides several hardware abstractions.

Let's look a bit deeper into the structures and functions of the main building blocks of an Arduino Uno: the Atmel ATmega328 microcontroller.

Block Diagrams

To understand how the software in the microcontroller blinks the LED, let's look at the block diagram of the ATmega328 microcontroller, shown in Figure 2-8. In general, understanding functional block diagrams is important when developing software for embedded devices.

The block diagram in Figure 2-8 shows the typical building blocks of a microcontroller. The CPU of the ATmega328 has an 8-bit instruction set. Instruction sets provide operations around which programmers build programming languages and compilers.

The code and data are stored in different forms of memory. In Figure 2-8, the memory is shown in the upper-right part. "Flash" generally means slow, nonvolatile memory, and SRAM means fast but volatile memory. You generally store programs in flash, while the RAM at runtime of a program is stored in SRAM.

Besides these building blocks, what is interesting from a software perspective are the interfaces of the microcontroller. These are all the arrows that come out and go in on the bottom and left—for example, the ports.

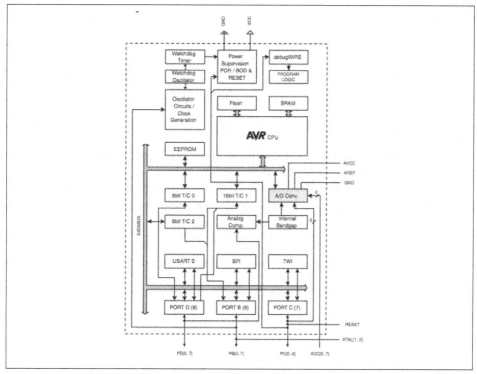

Figure 2-8. A functional block diagram of the datasheet from the ATmega 328 microcontroller

With GPIOs, it is possible to read and write data. From the block diagram, you can see that an Atmel MCU has GPIOs that are organized in three ports: Port B, Port C, and Port D (seen near the bottom of Figure 2-8).

So-called "peripherals" are also important for communication and sensing the outside world. Some peripherals act as input and output ports. Timers can measure the time between stop and start events. And, analog-to-digital converters can convert continuous analog signals into bits and bytes for digital processing.

The ATmega328 Atmel chip multiplexes the following blocks to the ports:

Port D provides USART and UART
> Many embedded devices must transfer data from one side to another. One kind of serial data transfer uses a Universal Synchronous Asynchronous Receiver/ Transmitter (USART). This peripheral function drives data bits from a sender to a receiver via two wires and an extra clock line. One variation on USART is called UART (Universal Asynchronous Receiver/Transmitter). In this form, a clock can be generated on the devices, and there is no need for an extra clock line. We'll discuss serial communication in several places throughout the book.

Port B provides SPI communication

Serial peripheral interface (SPI) is another approach to communicating between devices. SPI connects devices in a "master" and "slave" fashion.[2] This means one device controls the communication flow. This kind of communication is a relatively fast form of serial communication. The SPI protocol requires four signals for communication. Since it always uses a clock line, the communication happens synchronous.

Port C provides TWI

The ATmega328 includes another form of serial communication called a *two-wire interface* (TWI). It is more commonly known as I2C (*https://en.wikipedia.org/wiki/I%C2%B2C*) ("i squared c") and is popular for slow communication with sensors or displays. I2C uses one line for a clock signal, which means that I2C communication also happens synchronous.

Most communication modes are directly supported by JavaScript libraries. Serial communication is very common for many use cases. A JavaScript library for serial communication will be discussed in Chapter 8. Let's continue with pins that are important to sense the physical world around us.

Analog Inputs

Looking at the building blocks in Figure 2-8, we can see a rectangle "A/D conversion." Not all pins on the Arduino support reading analog values, only pins A0 to A5. The analog input block provides a number of "channels" to measure the physical environment with sensors.

In the Arduino language, these pins *read* a variable ("analog") voltage and report that value as a 10-bit number representing 0–5V. An analog value has a "continuous" value in a range, so it does not represent a state. The range is represented by a resolution with bits—for example, a 10-bit A/D converter has 2^{10} different values, or 1024 values (in hex values the range would be 0x00–0x3ff).

The simplest approach to understanding what happens when reading an analog input is with a potentiometer.

---

2 Pavel Boháčik, "MPC5121e Serial Peripheral Interface (SPI)" Freescale Semiconductor Application Note, 08/2009 (*http://cache.freescale.com/files/microcontrollers/doc/app_note/AN3904.pdf*)

Potentiometers are often used to adjust voltages, sound, or brightness, for example. They consist of a knob or a slider that you can adjust, which allows you to play with an analog voltage. You'll learn more about using electrical components in Chapter 7. But if you are confused right now, *Practical Electronics* by J. M. Hughes (O'Reilly, 2015) is a good resource for learning more about the basics of electronics.

If you connect a potentiometer to analog input A0 as shown in Figure 2-9, you can read the analog voltage on the input pin with:

```
board.analogRead(0, function(data) {
  console.log(data);
});
```

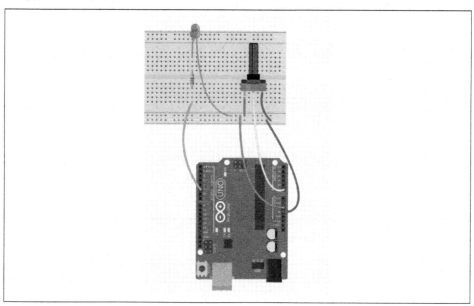

Figure 2-9. Potentiometer connected to analog input A0

You could influence the delay of the blinking LED on an Arduino as follows:

```
// analog_read.js
// load firmata dependency
var Board = require('firmata');

// pin definitions
const LED = 5;
const POT = 0;

// init variables
var ledOn = 0;  // whether LED is ON or OFF
```

```
var delay = 0;   // blink delay

// make connection
Board.requestPort(function(error, port) {

  if (error) {
    console.log(error);
    return;
  }

  var board = new Board(port.comName);

  // wait for connection
  board.on("ready", function() {

    function blink() {
      board.digitalWrite(LED, ledOn);
      ledOn = !ledOn;
      setTimeout(blink, delay);
    }

    // update variable
    board.analogRead(0, function(d) {
      delay = d;
    });

    blink();
  });
});
```

Often, you need to scale the input range of a sensor, or as in this example, the potenti-ometer (POT). In this case, the value from the analog pins returns a value between 0 an 1023. This values affects the delay for blinking.

When the blink delay is below 100 ms, the human eye cannot perceive the blink of the LED anymore. To map the blink delay to a range that can be seen by the human eye, you use a "map" function. The function from Arduino map (*http://arduino.cc/en/Reference/Map*) can be rewritten in JavaScript as follows:

```
function map(x, in_min, in_max, out_min, out_max)
{
    return (x - in_min) * (out_max - out_min) / (in_max - in_min) + out_min;
}
// e.g. map(value, 0, 1023, 400, 1600) --> maps a value in a range from 400 to 1600
```

Now, the full variable blink example reads:

```
// map_example.js
var Board = require('firmata');

// pin definitions
const LED = 5;
```

```
const POT = 0;

// init variables
var ledOn = 0;   // whether LED is ON or OFF
var delay = 0;   // blink delay

function map(x, in_min, in_max, out_min, out_max)
{
    return (x - in_min) * (out_max - out_min) / (in_max - in_min) + out_min;
}

// make connection
Board.requestPort(function(error, port) {

  if (error) {
    console.log(error);
    return;
  }

  var board = new Board(port.comName);

  // wait for connection
  board.on("ready", function() {

  function blink() {
    board.digitalWrite(LED, ledOn);
    ledOn = !ledOn;
    setTimeout(blink, delay);
  }

  // update variable
  board.analogRead(0, function(d) {
    delay = map(d, 0, 1023, 400, 1600);
  });

      blink();
    });
  });
```

If you turn the knob of the potentiometer to the left, you get a minimum blink delay of 400 ms. If you turn the knob to the right, the delay will be 1.6 s.

Pulse-Width Modulation

In many projects, you not only have the requirement to sense the environment, you will also need to *change* the environment. This is what actuators are about. An actuator can be a motor, a loudspeaker, or again, the blink of an LED.

Actuators respond to signals with different forms. Pulses with different widths are especially common. This modulation scheme is called *pulse-width modulation* (PWM). As you can see in Figure 2-10, you specify the percentage of the time that the signal is high, also known as the "duty cycle." This results in an often uneven square wave, as the pin approximates a percentage of the full signal by quickly toggling how long the signal is on versus off within a short period.

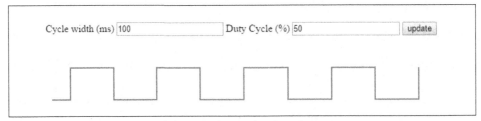

Figure 2-10. Pulse-width modulation; play with it here http://embeddednodejs.com/pwm

To generate PWM signals, a microcontroller often can often reuse exisiting blocks, such as GPIO and internal timers on the chips.

The mechanism behind PWM is as follows: an internal timer on the MCU sets the state of a pin to HIGH for a certain time, and LOW for the rest of a cycle. On *average*, the output is an analog voltage between ground and the supply voltage. This approximates an analog value and works fine for slow actuators. If you want fast-changing analog signals, such as needed for good quality audio, you'll need to explore the use of digital-to-analog converters (DACs). Unfortunately, simple Arduinos don't have DACs onboard.

Timing of Microcontrollers

Microcontrollers have many knobs to manage time-critical code. For example, the clock of a 16 MHz MCU can be configured to run slower to save power. Assuming that the processing of an instruction takes four clock cycles and the clock runs on 16 MHz, processing each instruction would take at least 250 ns. The human eye can only track changes above 100 ms, so we want some delay to execute the toggling of pin 13. This is why you call `delay` with some milliseconds as an argument.

The clock frequency of a microcontroller can be configured to run faster or slower. Generally, the higher the clock frequency, the more power a device consumes. For example, if your device runs on a battery, a slow MCU can be more interesting than a faster one. PJRC has a useful article about setting the system clock of an MCU (*https://www.pjrc.com/teensy/prescaler.html*). Timing again becomes important when you work with sample rates for analog-to-digital conversion or PWM.

Let's now get some practice using PWM to fade an LED. The Arduino example "fade" can be translated to JavaScript as follows:

```javascript
// analog_write.js
var Board = require('firmata');

// led pin
const LED = 5;

var brightness = 0;
var fadeAmount = 5;
Board.requestPort(function(error, port) {

if (error) {
   console.log(error);
   return;
}

var board = new Board(port.comName);
board.on("ready", function() {

// configure pin as PWM
board.pinMode(LED, board.MODES.PWM);

// fade the LED every 30 ms
function fadeLed() {
  brightness += fadeAmount;

     if (brightness == 0 || brightness == 255) {
        fadeAmount = -fadeAmount;
     }
     board.analogWrite(LED, brightness);
     setTimeout(fadeLed, 30);
   }
   fadeLed();
 });
});
```

A small warning: not every digital pin has access to a timer/counter. So, not every pin is able to drive a PWM output. On an Arduino, there are usually six pins with PWM functionality. These pins are commonly marked with a tilde.

Pinouts

Because reading functions of pins in datasheets is a time-intensive process, so-called *pinout diagrams*—like the one shown in Figure 2-11—help visualize pin functions.

While datasheets provide many details of what is going inside a chip, software developers are mostly interested in the interfaces of chips. To make writing embedded software easier, pinouts are a handy way to look up the names or locations of pins.

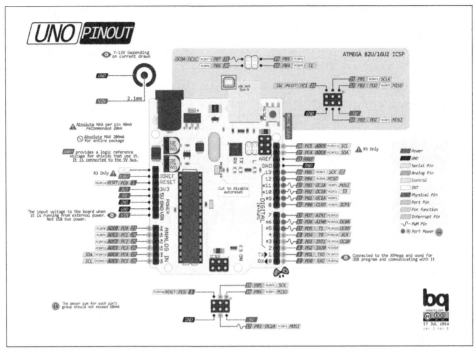

Figure 2-11. An Arduino Uno pinout that shows the location and functions of pins (http://www.pighixxx.com/test/pinouts/boards/uno.pdf)

From this pinout, we quickly get an overview of the different pin functions. In addition to the pin mapping that Arduino libraries use, you'll see the name of the lower-level name and function from the datasheet. For example:

```
Arduino Pin 9 | Physical Pin 15 | Port B | Output/Compare/Timer 1
```

For beginners of embedded development, consulting a pinout can be simpler than reading dense datasheets. Later, when you get more familiar with a microcontroller, you can explore the alternative functions of pins in a pinout or datasheet.

PighiXXX provides pinout diagrams for a number of popular Arduino boards (*http://www.pighixxx.com/test/pinoutspg/boards/#prettyPhoto*).

Firmware

Software inside an embedded device is also called *firmware*. After firmware is built and uploaded, a microcontroller knows what to do.

When using JavaScript for embedded devices, we often can simplify our lives by skipping custom firmware in C or C++. But a lot of software for hardware is written in C. It can be helpful to understand how custom firmware development works.

Firmware is stored in the "nonvolatile memory" (NVM) of a microcontroller, sometimes referred to as ROM. Changing programs in NVM is commonly called "flashing" a device. Flashing a device often requires a special programming device or a "programmer." To make programming devices easier, many boards support at least some flashing of NVM via USB.

The NVM can be organized into different address spaces. A small address space is reserved for the bootloader of a microcontroller. Similar to the BIOS inside a desktop computer, a small part in NVM is reserved for booting the device. This part of firmware is also called the "bootloader" and is independent from an application or "user code." In the case of Arduino, the bootloader starts up the Arduino and checks for programming requests from the outside.

For security reasons, flashing a bootloader via USB is often not possible. As long as your embedded code on an Arduino does not hit the wall of 32 KB, tinkering with the bootloader is often not required either.

Developing firmware is often highly dependent on which microcontroller you use. First, you need to choose the appropriate tools and compilers. Compiling a program for an AVR-compatible microcontroller is different from programming an ARM device or an x86. Then, writing compiled programs into the flash memory often requires special "programming tools." The tool that does this for Arduino is called *avr-dude*. A popular tool for ARM-based microcontrollers is *openocd*.

To use JavaScript with embedded devices, you usually build some kind of bridge layer, such as the Firmata protocol or Tessel 2 firmware (*https://github.com/tessel/t2-firmware*). Alternatively, you can build your own bridge with JavaScript to an embedded device based on serial communication.

In this book we haven't talked much about JavaScript on an embedded device yet. This is going to change in the next chapter on Espruino. Espruino improves on the Arduino experience in that you don't need to compile sketches, but can run JavaScript on the board itself.

## CHAPTER 3

Espruino

Espruino (*http://www.espruino.com*) is a "mini Node.js" for microcontrollers. It eliminates the need for a translation layer like Firmata with Arduino.

The Espruino project by Gordon Williams was funded via a Kickstarter campaign in 2014 and has been continuously improved since. To run JavaScript code on Espruino, you don't need to install an IDE or specific device drivers. You can use the Espruino Web IDE or use a simple serial terminal to program a device.

Similar to Arduino, Espruino has both hardware and software components. Espruino boards have a strong microcontroller core (a 32-bit ARM Cortex processor), and are faster and provide more memory (64–96 KB RAM and 256–512 KB flash) than an Arduino Uno. The better MCU is needed in order to parse JavaScript and libraries.

Espruino is completely open source. A variety of ports of the Espruino runtime have been made to other boards and processors. For example, boards with an ESP8266 are now supported. Although boards with an ESP8266 are popular due to cost and performance considerations, in order to support further development of the Espruino project, it is a good idea to buy the Espruino directly from the Espruino website.

The Espruino Hardware

On the hardware side, there are two main flavors: the original Espruino board (Figure 3-1) and the Espruino Pico (Figure 3-2). To quickly get started, the Espruino Pico (*http://www.espruino.com/Pico*) (around $30) is a good option. As you can see in Figure 3-1, there are several digital and analog pins. Compared to Arduino, the Pico has more pins to support PWM.

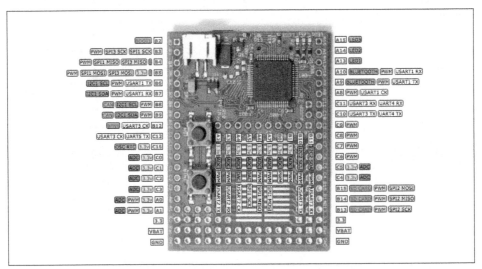

Figure 3-1. *The Original Espruino pinout from http://www.espruino.com/Espruino Board*

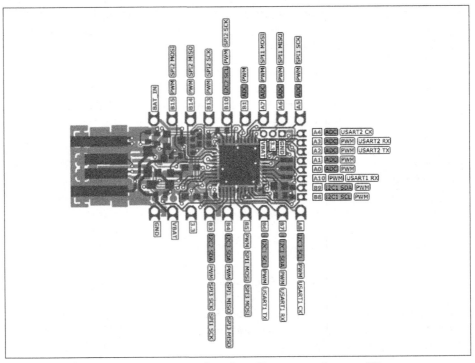

Figure 3-2. *The Espruino Pico pinout from http://www.espruino.com/Pico*

A good way to learn about JavaScript on Espruino is with a simple blinking LED. For this example, you can mount a Pico with an LED and resistor on a breadboard, as shown in Figure 3-3, between pin B3 and GND. (If you are new to electronics: breadboards and components will be discussed in Chapter 7.)

Figure 3-3. An Espruino Pico on a breadboard

To explore the analog pins, you can add a potentiometer to analog input pin A5, as shown in Figure 3-4.

Figure 3-4. An Espruino Pico with LED and potentiometer

Instead of a breadboard setup, you can mount an Espruino on a special board called a shim, which makes it easier to attach devices. You can purchase a shim collection (*http://www.espruino.com/Shims#shim-collection*) containing various shims for your Pico. Also, there is an adapter board ("Arduino Shim") to make an Espruino pin compatible with the Arduino form factor.

For software engineers without much soldering experience, it's worthwhile to take a look at Espruino's support (*http://www.espruino.com/Grove*) of Grove headers. This allows you to add the Espruino Pico to the Arduino Shim and plug it straight into the Grove header.

Because Espruino is an open source project, you can study the Espruino board designs to build your own Espruino-compatible devices. For example, the Eagle CAD outlines for the Pico can be found at *http://www.espruino.com/Pico#embedding-the-pico*.

Programming Espruino

For programming with Espruino, check out the tutorial at *http://www.espruino.com/Quick+Start* first. Linux and Mac OS X users can just plug in the board. Windows users might need to install a driver.

Espruino comes with an open source web IDE, as shown in Figure 3-5. The source code of the WebIDE can be downloaded from *https://github.com/espruino/Espruino WebIDE*. The WebIDE talks with the Espruino hardware via the Chrome serialport library. This means you are able to program the Espruino with JavaScript directly from a web browser!

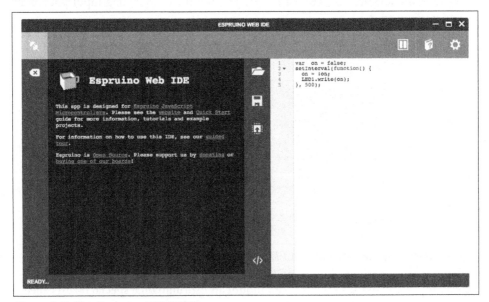

Figure 3-5. The Espruino WEB IDE

Besides support to upload JavaScript code on an Espruino, you can also control the device with a REPL. Figure 3-6 shows how you connect the Espruino to the web IDE.

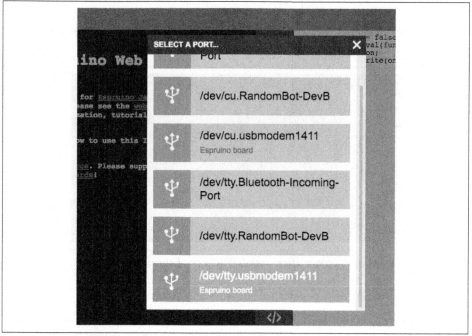

Figure 3-6. Connect to an Espruino

Once connected, you can turn the LED on B3 ON with:

```
> digitalWrite(B3, HIGH);
```

And OFF with:

```
> digitalWrite(B3, LOW);
```

Instead of LOW and HIGH, you can also simply use 0 and 1.

In addition to web IDE, you can also use serial communication to blink the LED. For this, you connect to the Espruino with a terminal program.

To use the Espruino command-line interface, you must install it first with:

```
$ npm install -g espruino-cli
```

If you want to use a terminal program, a good terminal for Mac OS X and Linux is screen (*https://www.gnu.org/software/screen*), while "hterm" is a popular choice on Windows machines.

For example, on Mac OS X, you can connect to the Espruino from the command line using screen:

```
$ screen /dev/cu.usbmodem141 9600
```

Once you are connected, you should see the welcome screen shown in Figure 3-7. In the REPL, you can run the same commands as from the WebIDE.

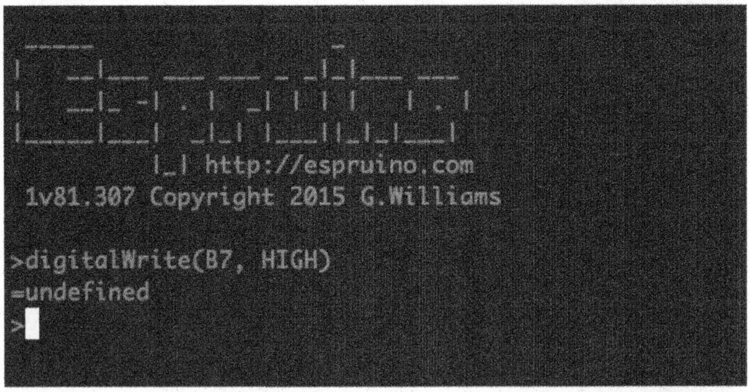

Figure 3-7. The welcome screen after connecting to the Espruino

Let's compare the Espruino experience so far with an Arduino.

We can make the following observations: first, the Espruino has built-in JavaScript functions to talk with the pins of the microcontroller. These JavaScript functions look similar to the Arduino—take digitalWrite, for example.

Second, the Espruino provides a read-eval-print loop (REPL) by default. With this, you can easily control electronic signals without compiling and flashing the device all the time. The REPL will be used a number of times in the book. The Espruino gives you a good start here.

Finally, Espruino programs do not have a main loop. Instead, you can use the event loop from JavaScript to run programs endlessly.

For example, to blink an LED endlessly, you can call setInterval():

```
var ledOn = false;
function blink() {
  ledOn = !ledOn;
  LED1.write(ledOn);
  console.log(ledOn);
}
setInterval(blink, 500);
```

Every 500 ms, there will be a call to the blink function. The event loop will run as long as the device has power.

Instead of setInterval, you can invoke a counter recursively with setTimeout:

```
var ledOn = false;
var delay = 500;
function blink() {
  digitalWrite(LED, ledOn);
  ledOn = !ledOn;
  setTimeout(blink, delay);
}
blink();
```

 If you want to do something every second, it's better to use setInterval, which is more accurate. Using setTimeout adds the time it takes to execute JavaScript code to each iteration.

Espruino also provides a function called digitalPulse to work with a timer directly. In this case, you can blink an LED with:

```
digitalPulse(LED1,1,delay);
```

When you write code as a series of small functions, the event loop can help you to process things almost in parallel. With the following JavaScript functions from the Espruino API (*http://www.espruino.com/Reference*), the Espruino interpreter can appear to do many things at once:

setTimeout
  Emit an event to call a function once after a specified length of time

setInterval
  It is like setTimeout but repeats

setWatch
  For checking input pin changes

Serial1.on(*data*, function() {})
  Subscribe to events when data comes in

An example of an event-based application is the REPL. This small process runs as just another *task*, effectively responding to USB.on('data'...) events.

Also, doing work only when an event happens can help you save power. If you use setInterval(.., 60000) then for 99.99% of that minute, Espruino can be totally asleep, saving a bunch of power.

By comparison, on an Arduino the default behavior is an endless loop() over the main program. With this, the Arduino never knows when the MCU is busy or when it isn't. The microcontroller of Arduino can't fall asleep automatically unless you explicitly tell it to.

When the board is ready, you can subscribe to the onInit event. This is comparable to the setup() function of Arduino.

Note that when you save or upload a program, Espruino saves the current state of the interpreter (not the code that you uploaded).

Variable Blink

Instead of defining a blink delay in the program, let's look at reading a delay time from a user via a potentiometer, as shown in Figure 3-4.

Assuming a potentiometer on the analog input pin A5, with:

```
var delay = 400 + 600 * analogRead(A5);
```

analogRead returns a value between 0 and 1. Compared to Arduino (which returns a value from 0 to 1024), you can just multiply this value to a maximum range value as you need it.

Adjust the blink frequency with the variable delay:

```
setInterval(function() {
  var delay = 400 + 600 * analogRead(A5);
  digitalWrite(LED1,1);
  setTimeout(function() {
    digitalWrite(LED1,0); },
  delay);
}, 1000);
```

Instead of adjusting the blink frequency, you can adjust the brightness of the LED with analogWrite:

```
setInterval(function() {
  var brightness = analogRead(A5);
    analogWrite(LED1,delay);
  }, 100);
```

Depending on the board and pins you want to use for PWM, you must enable a software PWM signal. Software PWM can be enabled by adding a parameter to analog Write: (LED1,delay,{soft:true});.

Modules

Espruino supports working with JavaScript objects, modules from npm, and special Espruino modules.

To load a module, you simply write in the editor pane of the web IDE:

```
var _ = require('concat-string');
```

The web IDE will automatically look up the module from npm. You can also load JavaScript drivers for many components from the Espruino repository. For example, to work with a display, you can require a module as described at *http://www.espruino.com/PCD8544*. A full example for a small animation on a display can be found at *http://www.espruino.com/Pico+LCD+Hello+World*.

Flashing Espruino Firmware

The Espruino firmware is continuously improving. To check the firmware version, click the setting button in the web IDE and scroll down to see the firmware version. For firmware updates, see *http://www.espruino.com/Quick+Start#software-updates*.

You can get the latest version of Espruino in a ZIP file from the Espruino download page (*http://www.espruino.com/Download*). The firmware is tested and you should use the *combined* version.

As mentioned earlier, you can install the Espruino firmware on other boards. Interesting boards include ESP8266-based boards or the BBC MicroBit (*http://www.espruino.com/MicroBit*). For this, you can use a Flash utility written in Node.js: *https://github.com/thingsSDK/flasher.js*.

## CHAPTER 4

The Tessel 2

OK, so you can blink from the command line and via Firmata or Espruino, but how about running full Node.js on a board? This is what a Tessel allows you to do.

Besides full Node.js compatibility, the Tessel board is great to get started working with the embedded Internet. The Tessel 2 hardware combines a microcontroller with a *system-on-a-chip* (SoC) that includes all-important building blocks for routing data in a network.

Hardware

The Tessel 2 is shown in Figure 4-1. The Tessel 2 combines a microcontroller with a more powerful microprocessor.

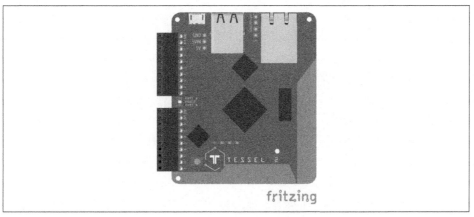

Figure 4-1. The Tessel T2 board from Rick Waldron's "Examples with fritzing diagrams" (https://github.com/rwaldron/tessel-io/tree/master/fritzing)

The idea of combining microcontrollers with a microprocessor is similar to the distributed nervous system of your body. The brain (processor) does the complex thinking, while other nervous centers in the body (controllers) coordinate the actions of hands, arms, and legs at the speed you need to react.

The "brain" in the Tessel 2 is the main processor with an operating system. Tessel 2 uses a 580 MHz Mediatek MT7620n SoC, a chip commonly found in WiFi routers. The Tessel main processor is powerful enough to run Node.js. It has 64 MB DDR2 RAM and 32 MB flash to store applications. For connectivity, there is 802.11bgn WiFi and an Ethernet port for an ultra-reliable wired connection.

For electronic peripherals, the nervous backbone of Tessel is an Atmel SAMD21 microcontroller that runs on 48 MHz, supports real-time I/O, and has an operation mode for low power. Tessel 2 is a completely open source project, so all of its hardware and software files are freely available online. You can find a guide to the tech stack here: *https://tessel.gitbooks.io/t2-docs/content/Debugging/Technical_Over view.html*.

Three advantages of the Tessel are:

- It surfaces all hardware features directly to JavaScript
- You can write code for a web server or other network protocols directly with Node.js libraries
- It lets you easily deploy scripted code using a text editor and the command line, the tools web developers already use every day

As shown in Figure 4-2, you can extend a Tessel with "modules." Tessel modules will be discussed in Chapter 7, which covers components for prototyping.

Figure 4-2. The Tessel T2 with a breakout board module and breadboard

There was also a Tessel 1, which was one of the first devices that could run JavaScript natively. While this approach was promising at first, the lack of compatibility with libraries from the Node.js ecosystem was seen as a disadvantage. To examine the strategy of this approach, there is a detailed overview of Tessel 1's software architecture at *https://github.com/tessel/t1-contribution-guide*.

Toolchain

As with selecting microcontrollers, toolchains play a role in the speed at which you can prototype systems. Based on JavaScript, the Tessel 2 toolchain offers a great experience to work with the embedded Internet.

Let's look first at what makes the Tessel experience so appealing. First, there is the Tessel command-line interface (CLI) that helps with managing a device. You can quickly upload code, configure network settings, or upgrade the firmware.

If you build systems with dozens of devices or want to create and manufacture a product on Tessel, cost can quickly become important. Tessel's eventual vision is to build tools that help users replace JavaScript with Rust or C as systems scale. It should be possible to just extract smaller hardware modules from a prototype before it goes into production. You can find an early draft of this workflow at *https://github.com/technicalmachine/fractal-docs*.

Command-Line Interface

Install Tessel 2's CLI with:

```
$ npm install -g t2-cli
```

Then plug in your Tessel 2 to your computer using USB. If you are using the Tessel 2 for the first time, the starting tutorial (*http://tessel.io/start*) is a good place to learn about the setup. You should give your Tessel 2 a name and allow provisioning from the computer that you use for development.

To check that your Tessel 2 is connected properly, you can type:

```
$ t2 list
```

Let's start a fresh project to blink an LED. In the directory where you want to work (perhaps make a new folder), type:

```
$ t2 init
```

This fills out the folder on your computer with a standard Node *package.json* and a file called *index.js* that contains the blinking LED example.

Here's the simplest version of a blinking LED example on Tessel 2:

```
// import the interface to Tessel hardware using the standard Node "require"
var tessel = require('tessel');

// blink!
setInterval(function () {
  tessel.led[2].toggle();
}, 100);
```

That's it! Requiring "tessel" in Node.js gives you access to the JavaScript API for the board's hardware. With the help of the `tessel` JavaScript library, you get objects and functions that can be performed on hardware such as an LED (see the full hardware API at *https://tessel.io/docs/hardwareAPI*). You can toggle this LED object. Internally, the Tessel firmware maps the LED name to a path in the OpenWRT filesystem.

To make this code run on Tessel 2, run the following command:

```
$ t2 run index.js
```

After you press Enter, you will see the following output:

```
INFO Looking for your Tessel...
INFO Connected to hellotessel.
INFO Building project.
INFO Writing project to RAM on hellotessel (3.072 kB)...
INFO Deployed.
INFO Running index.js...
I'm blinking! (Press CTRL + C to stop)
```

The `t2 run` command tells your computer to find your Tessel (either over USB or over your LAN), gain root access, copy over any necessary files from your directory, and then run your entry point file.

One of the LEDs on your Tessel 2 should now be blinking!

You can push the code over more permanently. Instead of `t2 run`, you can write:

```
$ t2 push
```

With this command, you can keep the same code between power cycles. This lets you unplug your Tessel and change it to a different power source, such as a battery.

You can also reprogram your Tessel while it is connected to a battery, as long as you are authorized (with the `t2 provision` command) and connected on the LAN.

You can also log in to your Tessel 2's Linux filesystem with the command:

```
$ t2 root
INFO Looking for your Tessel...
INFO Connected to hellotessel.
INFO Starting SSH Session on Tessel. Type "exit" at the prompt to end.

BusyBox v1.23.2 (2016-04-07 13:52:07 EDT) built-in shell (ash)
```

```
Tessel 2  /  Built on OpenWrt
root@hellotessel:~#
```

From here, you can explore the OpenWRT filesystem. Also, if you need to debug a setup, root access to the Tessel 2 can be helpful. An extended list of commands is available at *https://gist.github.com/flaki/a1efdb438292dd8c56c3*.

Another very useful function is to turn the Tessel 2 into a WiFi access point:

```
$ t2 ap -n SSID -p PASS
```

Using this method, you can manage multiple edge devices with a single Tessel 2.

Pin Abstractions

On a Tessel 2, the pins for physical computing are provided by an Atmel SAMD21. This microcontroller provides timers, analog-to-digital converters, and other peripherals. To learn about these building blocks with JavaScript, you can attach an LED to a module pin. This discussion is limited to digital and analog pins. A full list of hardware abstractions can be found at *https://tessel.io/docs/hardwareAPI*.

Digital Pins

On a Tessel, pinMode configuration (input vs output) happens implicitly whether you read or write to a pin. Take a look at this example in JavaScript:

```
var tessel = require('tessel');

var pin0 = tessel.port.B.pin[0];
var pin1 = tessel.port.B.pin[1];

// pin0 acts as output when you write data to it
pin0.output(1);

// pin1 acts as input when you read data from it
setInterval(function () {
  pin1.read(function(err, val) {
      console.log(val);
  });
}, 600);
```

Writing to pin0 is done with the function pin0.output(…). Reading digital data is done with pin1.read(…) pin functions.

Analog Pins

To work with analog signals, you can use analogRead(…) and analogWrite(…).

```
pin.analogRead(function(error, value) {
  console.log(value);
});
```

This can be used easily for fading an LED with a potentiometer, as was shown in earlier chapters.

For writing an analog value there, use `analogWrite(…)`. However, analog write can only be used on Pin 7 of Port B currently.

Embedded Internet with System-on-Chip

The combination of a microcontroller with SoC in a Tessel 2 is a great way to develop and prototype products for the IoT.

To run network services and web applications, the Mediatek SoC uses a microprocessor from the MIPS24k family.[1] This microprocessor uses a 32-bit instruction set that reduces program size and increases execution speed. The building blocks of the main Tessel chip are shown in Figure 4-3.

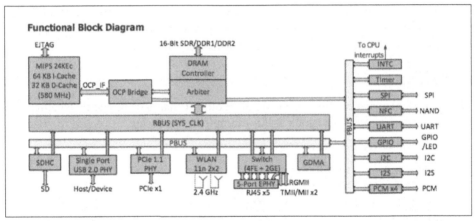

Figure 4-3. The functional blocks of a Mediatek MT7620 from the MIPS Technologies Software User's Manual (https://people.freebsd.org/~adrian/mips/MD00343-2B-24K-SUM-03.11.pdf)

You can quickly see the differences in blocks compared to the microcontroller from the previous chapters. To provide Internet access, the SoC has a powerful microprocessor that runs MIPS 24K and comes with integrated building blocks for WiFi and Ethernet. This makes the chip popular in many Internet gateways and WiFi routers.

---

1 The user manual: "MIPS32® 24K® Processor Core Family Software User's Manual", MIPS Technologies, Inc., December 19, 2008 (*https://people.freebsd.org/~adrian/mips/MD00343-2B-24K-SUM-03.11.pdf*).

Reduced Instruction Set Computers (RISC)

The MIPS technology was one of the first commercially available "reduced instruction set" computers, or RISC machines. RISC machines are often found in computers for special purposes (e.g., communication gateways) or for mobile applications. As its names states, RISC machines employ few instructions to run a program. By using "reduced" instructions, RISC processors are usually cheaper than their counterpart "complex instruction set computing," or CISC machines. The founder of the MIPS company is Professor John H. Hennessy, an important researcher in computer architecture and president of Stanford University.

With the SoC, the Tessel 2 provides many features for the development of connected devices out of the box. For example, you don't need to flash an SD card and install its image on the device. After unboxing the Tessel 2, you are ready to start programming with JavaScript right away. An image of OpenWRT comes preinstalled on the 32 MB flash memory that is connected to the SoC.

The OpenWRT image abstracts away much of the physical layer's complexity. You can find the build steps to build your own images of the Tessel 2 at *https://github.com/tessel/openwrt-tessel*.

The Tessel OpenWRT image also includes the Node.js runtime out of the box. You can see all packages of the distribution at *https://github.com/tessel/openwrt-tessel/blob/master/config.mk*.

Once you power on the Tessel 2 and connect via USB, you can configure the WiFi connection with a single command:

```
$ t2 wifi -n <network-name> -p <password>
```

Once you have configured the network, you can upload new code to the Tessel over a LAN connection. The following command line instruction explicitly pushes code over LAN:

```
$ t2 push --lan index.js
```

You should be able to see the device even with the USB cable removed.

To use JavaScript with embedded devices, you usually build some kind of bridge layer, such as the Firmata protocol or the Tessel 2 firmware (*https://github.com/tessel/t2-firmware*). Alternatively, you can build your own bridge with JavaScript to an embedded device based on serial communication or by using a custom protocol as the Tessel firmware shows (*https://github.com/tessel/t2-firmware/tree/master/firmware*). The microcontroller firmware communicates with network services through the OpenWRT operating system.

Running JavaScript and Node.js on embedded devices is a challenge that has inspired several approaches for both MCUs and MPUs. The differences can be in the chips chosen, the languages used, and the methods implemented to translate between the high-level language of JavaScript and the low-level communication needed by the electronic components. Two approaches (and their pitfalls) are presented in Jon McKay's Web Rebels 2016 talk, "The Eternal Struggle: Node.js in Embedded Devices" (*http://opbeat.com/ community/posts/the-eternal-struggle-node-js-in-embedded-devices- by-jon-mckay*). In particular, McKay explains the different languages and functions called at each layer of hardware abstraction.

## CHAPTER 5

Particle Photon

When cost or power put constraints on your hardware design budget, working with microcontrollers can be a relevant option. With a special transceiver chip for Internet access, boards such as the Particle Photon can, for example, act as sensor nodes in a room. Of interest to the book, much of the Particle toolchain is developed in Java-Script. This sets the background for this chapter.

The Particle (formerly Spark.io) family of boards talks to networks with different chips. The Photon board uses a WiFi chip from Broadcom (BCM43362) that handles the WiFi RF and protocol layer. Besides boards with WiFi, there are Particle boards that support 3G cellular networks.

The Particle Photon

From the perspective of the physical layer, an embedded device can either support Internet access on the same chip (as the Tessel 2 shows) or with specialized chips that handle the Internet connection.

In this chapter, let's look at a strategy to add building blocks for WiFi with an external chip such as the Particle Photon. The Particle Photon has a small form factor and low power consumption. But as with much of engineering, there are tradeoffs in selecting the "best" approach. From a JavaScript viewpoint, the Particle Photon is interesting because of its Node.js-based toolchain to develop applications with a Photon. The Particle Photon is shown in Figure 5-1.

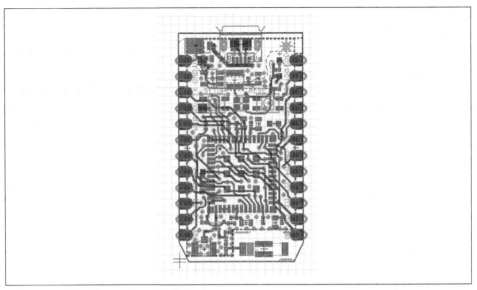

Figure 5-1. The Photon Particle board

While the WiFi chip handles Internet connectivity, an STM32 microcontroller handles the main application. The Particle boards use a "real-time operating system" FreeRTOS to manage device access and user code. With this approach, you can flash a Particle Photon with user code via the WiFi.

The boards from Particle are designed for products that are connected to the Internet. To improve the development experience for connected devices, Particle provides a web IDE (*http://build.particle.io*) to develop applications. With this platform, you can flash a device "over-the-air" (OTA). Alternatively, there is a downloadable IDE called Particle Dev, which is based on GitHub's Atom project.

 Particle and Arduino have some similar ideas about how open source communities can support innovation and product development. Similar to Arduino, you can find Particle board layouts on GitHub. Sharing toolchains and layouts leads to new products. One such product that is compatible with both Arduino and the Particle Photon is the Redbear Duo from Redbear Labs (*http://redbear.cc/*). The Redbear Duo can be connected to the Particle cloud and can be programmed with the Arduino IDE.

The Particle cloud and boards come with a cloud-based messaging platform that lets you easily send messages to—and from—the devices in a secure way regardless of where you are. That platform is included for free.

The current Particle boards support different libraries from the Arduino ecosystem. But Particle is not a completely Arduino-compatible product; you can't (yet) use the Arduino IDE, and Particle products have a different footprint. The boards are more similar to an Arduino Nano than Uno.

Many of the tools in the Particle toolchain are based on Node.js. Let's review how that works.

Particle Command-Line Interface

First, you must install the Particle command-line tools via npm. This is done with:

```
$ npm install -g particle-cli
```

With this, you have access to your particle via USB:

```
$ particle

Welcome to the Particle Command line utility!
Version 1.9.1
https://github.com/spark/particle-cli

Usage: particle <command_name> <arguments>
Common Commands:

setup, list, call, get, device, identify, flash, subscribe
compile, monitor, login, logout, help

Less Common Commands:
    token, binary, cloud, config, function, keys, serial, udp
    update, variable, webhook, wireless

For more information Run: particle help <command_name>
```

Next, you must set up the board, with the setup command:

```
$ particle setup
```

```
> Setup is easy! Let's get started...
> It appears as though you are already logged in as hello@embeddednodejs.com
? Would you like to log in with a different account? No
```

One indicator of the state of the board is the blink of the RGB color LED:

```
! PROTIP: Hold the MODE/SETUP button on your device until it blinks blue!
! PROTIP: Please make sure you are connected to the Internet.
```

Then you get asked some questions about your Internet connection:

```
> I have detected a Photon connected via USB.
? Would you like to continue with this one? Yes
! The Photon supports secure Wi-Fi setup. We'll try that first.

? Found "Photon-PRVL". Would you like to perform setup on this one now? Yes

> Obtained magical secure claim code.

> Hey! We successfully connected to Photon-PRVL

> Now to configure our precious Photon-PRVL

> Wi-Fi Network: TheWiFi
> Password: letsconnect
> Security: WPA2 AES

? Would you like to continue with the information shown above? Yes

> Obtaining device information...
> Setting up device id 2B003.......
> Requesting public key from the device...
> Setting the magical cloud claim code...
> Telling the Photon to apply your Wi-Fi configuration...
> The Photon will now attempt to connect to your Wi-Fi network...
```

To check that your device is working, run the following:

```
$ particle list
<no name> [2b00350013473.....] (Photon) is online
  Functions:
    int digitalread(String args)
```

From now on, you can program your device via the web IDE.

OTA Code Deploys

After you have set up a Particle device, you can use the Particle platform build.particle.io (*https://build.particle.io*) to deploy code via the network. These wireless firmware updates are called "over-the-air" updates. A simple example is shown in Figure 5-2.

```
https://build.particle.io/build/56f6977a606234d82a000b17

hello-serial.ino
1    char publishString[40];
2
3    void setup() {
4        pinMode(D6, INPUT);
5    }
6
7    void loop() {
8        unsigned long now = millis();
9
10       if (digitalRead(D6)) {
11           unsigned nowSec = now/1000UL;
12           unsigned sec = nowSec%60;
13           unsigned min = (nowSec%3600)/60;
14           unsigned hours = (nowSec%86400)/3600;
15           sprintf(publishString,"%u:%u:%u",hours,min,sec);
16           Spark.publish("Button", publishString);
17       }
18
19   }

Flash successful! Please wait a moment while your device is updated...
```

Particle Devices

Photon

photon1   >

photon2   >

Duo

redbear1   >

ADD NEW DEVICE

Figure 5-2. *The platform build.particle.io allows you to update firmware over the air*

As a basic example for using the Particle toolchain, consider a simple button connected to the Particle Photon via Grove connectors, as shown in Figure 5-3.

Figure 5-3. *A Particle Photon with Grove headers*

You can use the following code to capture the input press and publish an event to the Particle cloud:

```
// publishTime.ino
char publishString[40];

void setup() {
    pinMode(D6, INPUT);
}

void loop() {
    unsigned long now = millis();

    if (digitalRead(D6)) {
      unsigned nowSec = now/1000UL;
      unsigned sec = nowSec%60;
      unsigned min = (nowSec%3600)/60;
      unsigned hours = (nowSec%86400)/3600;
      sprintf(publishString,"%u:%u:%u",hours,min,sec);
      Spark.publish("Button", publishString);
    }
}
```

Next, you must update the firmware on the Particle Photon. When you now press the button, you can see events from the boards in the dashboard of build.particle.io, as shown in Figure 5-4.

Figure 5-4. Events from a button press

The same events can be accessed through the Particle API from any web page.

Node.js for the ESP8266

Another popular approach to connecting a microcontroller to the Internet involves using ESP8266-based boards. This chip is one of the cheapest approaches to controlling physical objects through the Internet. However, the ESP8266 requires some more hardware skill and a bit more time to get started. For example, with some ESP8266 boards, you must solder special boards to flash the device and install a number of extra tools. Some projects, such as the NodeMCU, try to solve this problem.

If you want to explore ESP8266 development with Node.js, a good place to start is *https://github.com/thingsSDK/flasher.js*.

## CHAPTER 6

Single-Board Computers

In addition to boards with microcontrollers and system-on-chips, there is another category of hardware that supports running Node.js: single-board computers (SBCs). SBCs integrate computer peripherals such as graphics cards and embedded memory on a single board. These kinds of devices are more similar to your laptop or desktop PC than they are to an Arduino.

The Raspberry Pi is a well-known example of an SBC. Intel Edison is also an SBC, with integrated peripherals for WiFi and Bluetooth communication.

Working with an SBC often means that you need to put some effort into installing an operating system and configuring it to your network. Getting an SBC to boot can quickly become challenging. Luckily, you will find many users to share ideas and help online. If you have worked with web applications before, configuration of an SBC feels a bit similar to server administration.

When your operating system is booting and you have a working Internet connection, adding Node.js to the device is often the easy part.

The Raspberry Pi

Computers such as Raspberry Pi consume more current (300–500 mA) than a microcontroller (10–30 mA). To work with a Raspberry Pi, you must ensure that your power supply can handle the large current draw of the processor. In addition to a special power supply, you should also have an HDMI cable for adding a display and a USB keyboard to access the device.

Raspberry Pis offer relatively high computing power for network access and building multimedia experiences. By using an embedded Linux operating system, you can directly run Node.js (and other programming languages) on the device, but without a microcontroller component, you lose real-time control over the GPIOs. If you work with analog data from sensors or for driving a motor, you often must fall back to simple binary protocols and external chips. Still, the Raspberry Pi and others are very popular, as there are still a bunch of digital pins with 3.3V voltage level that can be used to control circuits.

The Raspberry Pi comes in different models: Model A, Model B, Model 2, the Zero, and Model 3. Most models support Internet connections by Ethernet and RJ45 cables. If you want to build wireless solutions, you must add WiFi USB dongles. For boards without Ethernet access (e.g., Model A and Zero), it is good to get a USB-to-Ethernet adapter.

Finding the IP Address of a Raspberry Pi

Some Raspberry Pis are configured to use the dynamic host controller protocol (DHCP) to get an IP address. This can make it difficult to find the Raspberry Pi after you plug it into your network.

Instead of login via a monitor and keyboard, you can find the IP address of a Raspberry Pi with some other tools.

For example, there is the nmap tool (*http://linuxcommand.org/man_pages/nmap1.html*) on Mac OS X and Linux. After installing it, you can use the following nmap command to search open ports in a range of network addresses:

```
$ nmap -p 22 --open -sV 192.168.2.0/24
```

This port scan will take a few seconds, but if everything works, you will see something along these lines:

```
Starting Nmap 6.46 ( http://nmap.org ) at 2014-07-13 14:10 CEST
Strange error from connect (65):No route to host
Nmap scan report for myrouter.ip (192.168.2.1)
Host is up (0.0024s latency).
PORT    STATE SERVICE VERSION
80/tcp open  http    Router HAD23V WAP http config
Service Info: Device: WAP

Nmap scan report for MYRPI (192.168.2.103)
Host is up (0.024s latency).
PORT    STATE SERVICE VERSION
22/tcp open  sshd
```

Another option is to install an app on your smartphone. There are several apps available that make it easier to manage a Raspberry Pi.

BeagleBone

The BeagleBone project was launched by Texas Instruments, DigiKey, and Element14 in 2008. BeagleBone boards have been revised a number of times already since the product's launch.

One of the most popular versions of BeagleBone is the BeagleBone Black. The board has an AM335 ARM Cortex A8 processor, 256 MB of RAM, and a clock frequency of 1 GHz. It has 2 GB of onboard flash memory.

The board has a number of peripherals, such as a micro-HDMI connector for video output and an SD card slot for external storage. It also has an Ethernet port for easy network connectivity. If you want to use WiFi, you must add a WiFi dongle, as shown in Figure 6-1.

Figure 6-1. The BeagleBone Black with a WiFi dongle

The board comes preloaded with a Debian Linux distribution. BeagleBone Black comes with a JavaScript runtime that is called BoneScript.

The BeagleBone supports multiple I2C and SPI busses. The newer and cheaper BeagleBone Green also has Grove headers for adding I2C devices.

In contrast to a Raspberry Pi, a BeagleBone has onboard ADC for analog-to-digital conversion.

To get started, you can follow the instructions available at "Getting Started with BeagleBone & BeagleBone Black" (*http://beagleboard.org/getting-started*).

The Intel Edison

The trend to build smaller, increasingly compact computers is ongoing. Intel introduced a "computer-on-module" with the Intel Edison in 2014. The module has an x86 Atom processor (the class found in tablet computers) and 4 GB embedded flash memory. This provides enough computing power to run network services or even a small database.

To see what "computer-on-module" means, have a look at the Edison datasheet (*http://download.intel.com/support/edison/sb/edisonmodule_hg_331189004.pdf*) to see how the module is built (Figure 6-2).

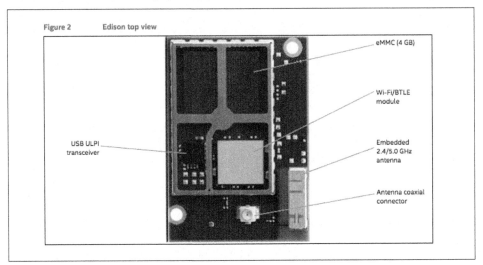

Figure 6-2. The Intel Edison module top

The main components are on top:

- eMMC (embedded memory)
- A WiFi transceiver with antenna: the Edison supports wireless connectivity out of the box. If you want to work with Ethernet, take a look at the Intel Galileo board (see "Intel Galileo" on page 231). That board is a bit older than the Edison, but can be interesting for smart home applications, e.g., where you have access to Ethernet.
- Bluetooth transceiver: Bluetooth will play an important role in the future of the Internet. We'll postpone the Bluetooth discussion until Chapter 15.
- USB transceiver

On the bottom of the module, there are the main processing blocks and a component for power management (Figure 6-3):

- Processor and DDR memory
- Power management IC (PMIC)
- A 70-pin Hirose connector

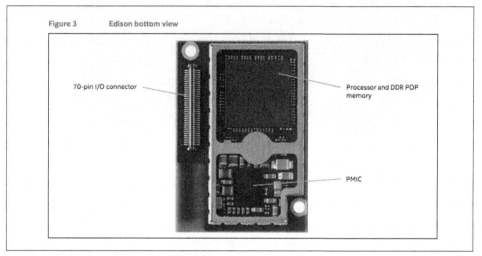

Figure 3   Edison bottom view

70-pin I/O connector

Processor and DDR POP memory

PMIC

Figure 6-3. The Intel Edison module bottom

With an Intel Edison, you can build highly integrated computers. But take note that the logical levels of the core processor are on 1.8V. On the one hand, this is nice for low-power consumption. On the other hand, this makes it harder to connect "classical" components made for an Arduino or Raspberry Pi.

To solve this problem for prototyping purposes, you can use so-called "breakout boards" (Figure 6-4). This will be discussed further in the next chapter. At this stage, let's briefly review how the software stack works on Edison.

While the Edison has an embedded flash memory with a default operating system, you will need to tune the operating system to your needs. In other words, you may wish to run a firmware update and install some extra packages on your Edison. Luckily, Node.js is preinstalled on the latest Yocto Linux images.

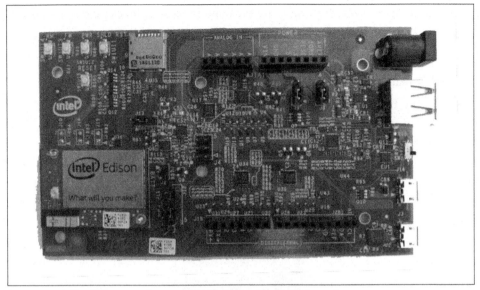

Figure 6-4. The Edison package on an Arduino breakout board

With a special breakout board from Tektyte, you can make the Intel Edison compatible to the header pins of a Raspberry Pi.

Figure 6-5. The Edison mounted on the Edi-Expand from Tektyte

---

Boards with 64-Bit Instruction Sets

If you need more performance on a single board, it makes sense to look at processors that support 64-bit instruction sets. These boards not only have processors with high performance, but also high-speed IOs for network or USB access. In the upper price range for SBCs, boards have an x86 processor where you can use the same software and operating systems as larger desktop computers.

The Upboard and Minnowboard Turbot, shown in Figure 6-6, are two examples of SBCs with x86 processors.

The Upboard (*http://up-shop.org*) was successfully funded through a Kickstarter campaign (*https://www.kickstarter.com/projects/802007522/up-intel-x5-z8300-board-in-a-raspberry-pi2-form-fa*). The board has Gigabit Ethernet and a 40-pin header that is compatible with a Raspberry Pi. It has 2 GB of RAM and 32 GB of embedded flash. The main community for this board can be found at *http://www.up-community.org/forum*. The price point is around $99.

The MinnowBoard Turbot is an open source hardware project based on a 64-bit Intel Atom system-on-chip. It has Gigabit Ethernet and a USB 3.0 port. The better performance of the board comes at the higher price of $145.

Figure 6-6. The Upboard (left) and Minnowboard Turbot (right) both use an x86 processor

If you are interested in more x86-based SBCs, check out Kickstarter—new boards are launched frequently.

Using Embedded Linux

An operating system such as embedded Linux is needed to capture the computing power of SBCs. This often requires that you prepare an SD card or USB memory stick first. After the operating system is installed, you will need to configure a network. Pending successful board setup, you can install and run Node.js inside an embedded device. If you are working with a Tessel 2, you will not need to do this; Node.js and the board's operating system come pre-installed.

Working with SD Cards

To run Node.js inside a board, you may have to prepare an SD card with an operating system and Node.js first. This is true for Raspberry Pi, Beaglebone, Upboard, and Intel Edison, among others. Let's look how this is done, and why it is needed.

Most boards require micro SD cards. With an adapter (shown in Figure 6-7), you can easily use the card in older (nonmicro SD) card readers or a Raspberry Pi model A too. It is a good idea to buy several SD cards of 4 GB or more from eBay so you can experiment easily with different settings and operating systems.

Figure 6-7. An SD card with adapter

Once you have the cards, you must download the image of an operating system.

When using a Raspberry Pi, you can download (*https://www.raspberrypi.org/down loads*) a Debian image. For Raspberry Pi, there are many articles that discuss how to install the image. For example, good instructions can be found here (*https:// learn.adafruit.com/adafruit-raspberry-pi-lesson-1-preparing-and-sd-card-for-your-raspberry-pi/downloading-an-image*).

When using an Intel Edison or Galileo, you can download the "IOT Kit SDK Image" from Intel.

Using a terminal or archive program, you can extract the image to a temporary location. To burn an image onto the SD card, you can copy blocks 1:1 from the source file to a destination drive.

When you are on Linux or Mac OS X, you can do this by using the dd command. You may need to check the location of your SD card in the filesystem and unmount it first. On a Mac, this can be done with:

```
$ diskutil list
$ diskutil unmountDisk /dev/diskN
```

N is the location of the card, such as 1, 2, or another drive.

 Be careful when using the dd command to flash an SD card from the command line. If you hit the wrong partition, you can format the wrong drive of your laptop.

Then, copy the image over to the SD card:

```
$ sudo dd if=iot-devkit-YYYYMMDDHHMM-mmcblkp0.direct of=/dev/disk1 bs=8m
```

Note that you copy the image directly onto the drive, not to a partition. This is important in order to obtain a card that can boot. bs specifies the "blocksize" for the copy process. Generally, an 8 MB block provides a good compromise between quality and speed of the copying process. Note that on some machines you must use a capital "M" for this (e.g., bs=8M).

Now that you have a board where we can install and run Node.js, let's review the role of the operating system.

Embedded Linux Distributions

There are different Linux distributions. One main parameter in choosing an operating system distribution is its size.

If you prepare an SD card for an Intel Galileo and boot from it, you'll see all kinds of processes running, as shown in Figure 6-8.

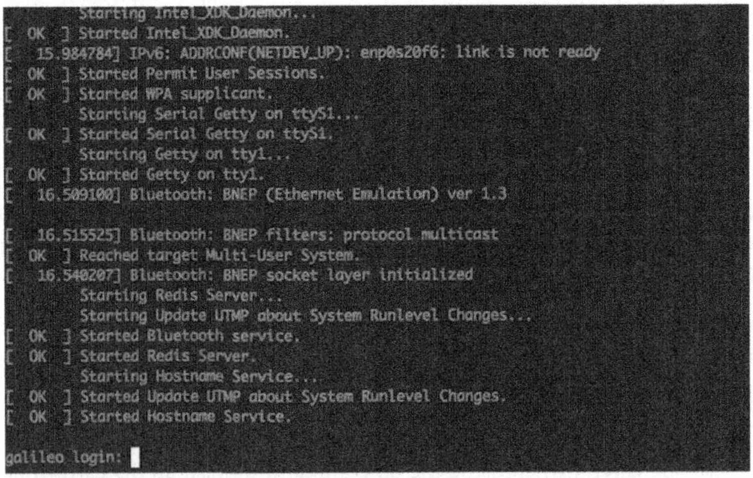

Figure 6-8. Booting a Galileo with the SD card image

Once an operating system is loaded, it manages the board's resources, including disk space, memory, and computing capacity.

When you then run a web server or a logger process for temperature, for example, you request resources from the operating system at different levels. Hardware resources are managed inside a "kernel." In Linux, these resources are mounted in the filesystem with "drivers" or "kernel modules."

In addition to providing better management of computing resources, operating systems often support running Node.js *inside* of an embedded system.

Because an operating system influences the way we develop with an embedded system and Node.js, let's briefly review some popular operating systems for embedded Node.js. This discussion is important to better understand board configuration.

OpenWRT

The history of OpenWRT is interesting. The company Linksys had to release its router firmware because it violated the GPL license of some Linux tools inside. The first public release of WRT to OpenWRT was in 2003.

With OpenWRT, it was possible for others to extend and configure router firmware as needed. One such project is Linino (*http://www.linino.org*), which can be found in the Arduino Yun project. Another offspring of OpenWRT is the Freifunk project, a community-driven wireless network approach. OpenWRT is at the heart of the Tessel 2 and Onion Omega development boards.

The package manager of OpenWRT is called *opkg* and is similar to Debian's *dpkg*. Node.js can be installed, for example, with:

```
$ opkg update
$ opkg install node
```

A number of Node.js modules are available for OpenWRT, such as *node-serialport*.

Debian

Debian is one of the Unix distributions that runs on many different kinds of hardware, from servers to desktop computers to embedded devices.

As a first step, it is often good advice to configure the connectivity of the device. This is done with some entries in the *networks* directory.

For users of the Raspberry Pi, a popular Debian distribution is the Raspbian distribution. For users of x86-embedded boards, such as an Intel Edison or UpBoard, a good choice is Ubilinux (*http://www.emutexlabs.com/ubilinux*).

Once installed, you can easily run the Aptitude package manager:

```
# apt-get update
```

To ensure scripts are started during startup, you can place links to scripts in the directory */etc/init.d/*.

Yocto

The Yocto project provides tools and packages specifically for embedded systems. The project was announced 2010.

The package manager of Yocto is "smart" (more information about "smart" is available in the blog post "Get smart with smart package manager" (*https://www.yoctopro ject.org/blogs/khem/2013/get-smart-smart-package-manager*)).

The Intel Edison runs Poky Linux image by default, which is based on a Yocto image. One difference from the Poky image to the Debian one is handling services. Poky uses the newer systemd (*https://en.wikipedia.org/wiki/Systemd*) to manage services and configurations of the board.

Network Configuration

To install packages from Node.js, it is often necessary to configure network access first. Network configuration is also important when you plan to develop systems with multiple devices.

A good start is to check whether you have network access or not. The Linux command that displays network information is:

```
$ ifconfig
```

The output may look like this:

```
enp0s20f6 Link encap:Ethernet  HWaddr 98:4F:EE:05:13:94
          UP BROADCAST MULTICAST  MTU:1500  Metric:1
          RX packets:0 errors:0 dropped:0 overruns:0 frame:0
          TX packets:6 errors:0 dropped:0 overruns:0 carrier:0
          collisions:0 txqueuelen:1000
          RX bytes:0 (0.0 B)  TX bytes:980 (980.0 B)
          Interrupt:49 Base address:0xc000

enp0s20f6:avahi Link encap:Ethernet  HWaddr 98:4F:EE:05:13:94
          inet addr:169.254.6.107  Bcast:169.254.255.255  Mask:255.255.0.0
          UP BROADCAST MULTICAST  MTU:1500  Metric:1
          Interrupt:49 Base address:0xc000

lo        Link encap:Local Loopback
          inet addr:127.0.0.1  Mask:255.0.0.0
          inet6 addr: ::1/128 Scope:Host
          UP LOOPBACK RUNNING  MTU:65536  Metric:1
          RX packets:480 errors:0 dropped:0 overruns:0 frame:0
          TX packets:480 errors:0 dropped:0 overruns:0 carrier:0
          collisions:0 txqueuelen:0
          RX bytes:37600 (36.7 KiB)  TX bytes:37600 (36.7 KiB)
```

This tells you the board has an Ethernet interface that is assigned the IP address 169.254.6.107. In most cases, you need to configure this address to fit your network. Let's look at how to do that.

You can assign a static IP address or get one dynamically. For a static IP address, you would add these lines in */etc/ifaces*:

```
auto eth0
iface eth0 inet static
    address 192.168.3.200
    netmask 255.255.255.0
```

A static IP address is a good idea for the first setup of a board. With a static IP address, you don't need to search the whole network for your device, but you can directly say:

```
$ ssh 192.168.3.200
```

You can also connect directly to your board through a USB-to-serial converting cable. You can run this line on the board:

```
$ ifconfig
```

Now, you'll see an IP address next to your MAC address of the network interface. You can share an Internet connection from a connected laptop with some steps (*https://*

vidotsh.wordpress.com/2014/11/25/sharing-laptop-Internet-connection-with-galileo-linux).

When using a WiFi network just for Internet access from the board, a dynamic IP address often is simpler. For this, you could add a WiFi network with DHCP by writing a few more lines in the network interface file:

```
auto wlan0
iface wlan0 inet dhcp
    wpa-ssid "mynetwork"
    wpa-psk  "sesameopen"
```

Now if you run:

```
# ifconfig
```

We see the basic subnet 255.255.255.0.

WiFi Configuration

If you need to inspect WiFi, it is good to look at the output of:

```
# iwconfig
```

You can find several interesting Node.js libraries related to WiFi configuration on *http://npmjs.com*. For example, to check from a script if a device has WiFi, there is the module node_wpa_cli (*https://github.com/afilini/node_wpa_cli*).

There are some special IP addresses—for example, 192.168.0.1, most routers' default IP.

Many humans prefer dealing with words rather than numbers. As such, a "domain name service," or DNS, helps to map IP addresses to domain names. To set the name of a device, you can use:

```
# hostname device1
```

To permanently change the hostname of a device, you must set the hostname in a file in */etc/hostname*.

To check that the hostname changed, write:

```
# hostname
upboard
```

After changing the hostname, it is a good idea to reboot the board. You can then check that the IP address of the device maps correctly to the new device name:

```
127.0.0.1    localhost.localdomain localhost
127.0.1.1    device1
```

Debugging Network Settings

Some Unix tools are especially helpful to debug network settings.

For example, you want to see what network services are running on the board. For this, you can use the Unix command:

```
$ netstat -tulpn
```

To see if you can reach some other device in the network, it can be helpful to "ping" the device. One of the best ways to understand what is going on is to simply ping a server:

```
$ ping google.com
```

You can also follow the route of packets with traceroute:

```
$ traceroute google.com
```

You can find more information at *http://www.unixdude.org/2012/12/use-traceroute-to-check-for-open-ports*.

Running Node.js

For the Linux distributions above, there is good support for Node.js.

For example, for Debian, you can install Node.js with its package manager *dpkg*. Another option is *aptitude*. Installing Node.js with *aptitude* is as simple as:

```
$ apt-get update
$ apt-get install nodejs
```

The Node Version Manager, nvm, is also supported on some boards.

Deploy Projects with Git

It can take patience to configure and boot an SBC to get the first LED to blink with JavaScript. With a complete filesystem and hardware for Internet, some more scripts and tools are useful.

A tool for version control can help to synchronize the state of a project between devices or to copy a project from your laptop to an embedded device. Basically, this does the same thing as the Tessel 2 commands from Chapter 4 (t2 run or t2 push).

If you are new to Git, take a look at *https://git-scm.com*. The basic commands are `git init`, `git add`, and `git commit`. Once you have added and committed code to a repository, you can track the project history with `git log`. What makes Git especially interesting is its capacity to work with remote repositories. You can easily apply the same concepts that you find at GitHub or Heroku to working with embedded devices.

First, on a remote device, let's initialize a bare Git repository. For example, on an Edison, this could look like:

```
$ ssh root@eddie.local
# mkdir -p git/led13.git && cd $_
# git init --bare
Initialized empty Git repository in /home/root/projects/buttons/git/led13.git/
```

A bare repository looks more like a database than a copy of a project. However, the bare repository can be addressed from other places, and once you update it, you can push changes automatically to copies of the repository.

Let's try this. First, you clone the bare repository on the device:

```
# cd projects
# git clone /home/root/git/led13.git
```

For automatic updates, let's create a post-receive hook for automatic deployment.

```
# cat > hooks/post-receive
#!/bin/sh

cd /home/root/projects/led13
unset GIT_DIR
git pull
echo "post receive finish"
```

The *post-receive* hook is executed as soon as there are new objects in the repository. In this example, we update the repository in */home/root/projects/led13* with a `git pull` command.

To let Git run the script, you must make it executable with:

```
# chmod u+x hooks/post-receive
```

Let's now test that this works by pushing a JavaScript file to the device via the repositories above.

First, clone the bare repository on your local machine:

```
$ git clone ssh://root@eddie.local:/home/root/git/led13.git
```

Next, let's init the project by creating a file *package.json*:

```
$ npm init
This utility will walk you through creating a package.json file.
It only covers the most common items, and tries to guess sensible defaults.

See `npm help json` for definitive documentation on these fields
and exactly what they do.

Use `npm install <pkg> --save` afterwards to install a package and
save it as a dependency in the package.json file.

Press ^C at any time to quit.
name: (inputs)
version: (1.0.0)
description:
entry point: (index.js)
test command:
git repository:
keywords:
author:
license: (ISC)
```

You can answer all questions with "yes" by running:

```
$ npm init -y
```

Next, you add this file to the repository with:

```
$ git add .
$ git commit -m "init"
$ git push origin master
```

You can see that after pushing the commit to the embedded device, the *post-receive* script is executed. If you now log in to that device and check the directory, you can check the latest commit with:

```
# git log
```

## CHAPTER 7

Components for Prototyping

The components you select define what hardware devices you can build. To add components to devices, it is important to understand how to build basic electronic circuits.

Circuits and components are the topics of this chapter. Because entire books are written about this (one important one is Paul Horowitz's *Art of Electronics* [Cambridge University Press, 2015]), the material we'll cover here focuses in particular on prototyping and experimentation on systems. The overview about electronic parts should also help you to better follow programming examples in later chapters.

If you are new to hardware, your first experiences with circuits and components can be daunting. In this case, you might want to learn with Tessel modules first. With Tessel modules (*https://tessel.io/modules*), you get circuits and components that you can plug into your Tessel without the pain (or joy) of debugging an electronic setup. You can easily make your own Tessel modules once you get familiar with electronics. If you do, you can share your new module with the Tessel community, and thousands of people around the world could benefit from your work.

Wiring Circuits

Working with embedded devices requires you to gain some understanding of underlying physics and electronics. These topics can be a lot of fun, but they often require adopting a different mindset than you might use when writing software.

Compared to software, building circuits is often expensive in terms of both time and money. Unlike software, you need to buy physical parts that cost money and must be shipped. Once the parts have arrived in your workspace, you must connect the parts to one another with different tools. Also, you can damage the parts if you build your circuits incorrectly.

While beginners can expect some frustrations with initial circuit design, building a working electronic device is very rewarding, too. Let's look into different ways of getting a physical circuit to work.

Breadboards

Breadboards provide a simple yet effective approach for learning about components and systems. They include premade connections that you can use to build basic circuits with jumper wires. In most cases, the breadboard provides vertical and horizontal connections. The outer part of a breadboard is then often used for supply voltages and a common ground.

 Want to learn more about breadboarding? Breadboard How-To (*http://www.instructables.com/id/Breadboard-How-To*) by Instructables user amandaghassaei is an introduction to the breadboard with exercises for an electronics beginner.

There are many examples of electronic circuits on a breadboard. For example, to build a simple input button, it is necessary to provide a default voltage to the input pin of a microcontroller. This can be done with the circuit shown in Figure 7-1 where a pull-down resistor prevents a floating input voltage.

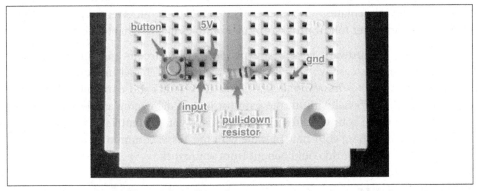

Figure 7-1. Simple switch on a breadboard

Building a circuit can take some time. On a breadboard, the more jumper wires and components you place, the more fragile a setup becomes. On the other hand, you don't need tools and skills for soldering if you use a breadboard, and you can get basic components working quickly.

Let's look at some other options for exploring circuits.

Grove Kit

For building circuits with a "plug and play" experience, the Grove Kits from Seeed Studio provide an interesting entry point (see Figure 7-2).

Figure 7-2. The Grove base shield (top right) provides headers to easily connect components (left and bottom)

The Grove kit is based on three ideas:

- A simple "base shield" in an Arduino form factor provides standard headers for cables
- Cables from components can then easily be plugged into the base shield
- Components such as a button, a potentiometer, some sensors, a buzzer, and a display with the same standard header connectors as the base shield

Compared with a breadboard, you'll easily have access to a button or potentiometer, for example. Instead of wiring up a button with a pull-up resistor as before, you'll now have a button component as shown in Figure 7-3.

Figure 7-3. A simple button from the Grove Starter Kit

You can solder Grove headers to your own boards too. Some boards, such as the BeagleBone Green, have Grove headers mounted by default already.

Besides the Arduino form factor, the Grove headers make customs setups a bit harder to design. For example, when you need multiple buttons or potentiometers, it is better to design and solder your own boards. But for many software developers, the Grove system is a good start to explore electronics for embedded software development.

Soldering

It can be fun to learn soldering and build components yourself. Components that arrive unsoldered to a breakout can be cheaper, and you have some more flexbility to make components as you need them. Additionally, for debugging a setup, learning to solder can be important. For example, an LED soldered to a resistor, such as the one in Figure 7-4, can often be helpful to quickly check the voltage on a pin.

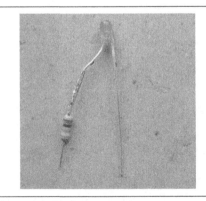

Figure 7-4. An LED with resistor for debugging

Because LEDs, resistors, potentiometers, and switches are used frequently, it is a good idea to purchase a number of them. You can make them easily pluggable or breadboardable by soldering jumper wires onto them.

Similarly, you can turn a potentiometer into a debugging tool by soldering jumper wires onto it. A potentiometer typically has three pins: GND, full scale, and a divided voltage. When working on a sensor device, this last pin is one you want to attach to an analog pin of a microcontroller. When you adjust the potentiometer, the divided voltage moves up or down an analog scale from ground (0V) to the full-scale voltage.

Figure 7-5. A potentiometer with jumper wires soldered onto it

Printed Circuit Boards

Soldering circuits with wires yourself quickly becomes time consuming for larger circuits. In these situations, a good option is to move to printed circuit boards (PCBs).

Many vendors such as SparkFun or Adafruit offer PCBs including a schematic of the board and the board layout including the used parts. Besides companies that promote open source hardware, a good place to find PCBs is at OSHpark (*https://oshpark.com/shared_projects*), Tindie (*https://www.tindie.com*), or GitHub.

With computer programs such as Eagle or Kicad, you can easily adapt PCBs to your own needs. This is a two-phase process. First, you capture a circuit in a schematic editor. Then you turn the schematic into a layout that can be manufactured. For boards with two layers, you can order boards for less than $10 at places like OSHpark (*https://oshpark.com*) or DirtyPCBs.

While learning PCB design takes some time, it will save time later when you start building more complicated hardware devices. This can already be seen from the number of wires on a simple breakout board with LEDs, as shown in Figure 7-6.

Figure 7-6. LEDs on a breakout board on a breadboard (you can find a simple PCB doing the same thing at https://oshpark.com/shared_projects/ZsQu0dA9)

For prototyping, breakout boards with small circuits to accompany components are especially useful. Breakout boards make components easier to access and often provide some basic configuration for components. Breakout boards not only work with "simple" components, but also with advanced components such as microprocessors and microcontrollers. For example, to turn the small pins of an Intel Edison into something useful for prototyping, a number of interesting boards, such as the ones pictured in Figure 7-7, can be used. The boards shown here were purchased from SparkFun.

For some boards, such as the Arduino Uno or a BeagleBone, there exist special boards that you can plug onto the "motherboard." This idea of an Arduino shield is nicely explained at the Arduino website (*https://www.arduino.cc/en/Main/ArduinoSh ields*):

> Shields are boards that can be plugged on top of the Arduino PCB extending its capabilities. The different shields follow the same philosophy as the original toolkit: they are easy to mount, and cheap to produce.

These shields (or "capes" for BeagleBone) can be very interesting for prototyping. If you want to focus purely on software development, these boards allow you to avoid thinking about circuit design almost completely.

A nice example for an Arduino shield is shown in Figure 7-8. This Arduino Uno–compatible shield provides a number of components, such as a real-time clock, temperature sensor, and input buttons. The board was designed by Dan Hienzsch and was funded with a Kickstarter campaign (*https://www.kickstarter.com/projects/ 1080546871/the-i2c-and-spi-education-system*).

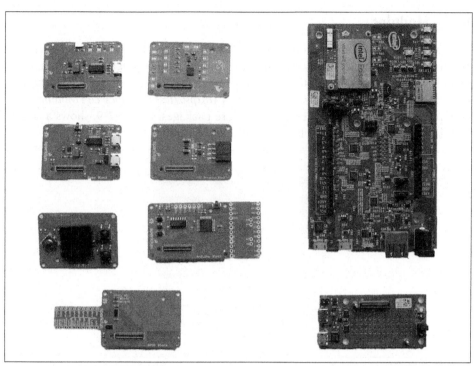

Figure 7-7. Some examples of breakout boards for the Intel Edison from SparkFun (in red)

Figure 7-8. The I2C education shield (https://rheingoldheavy.com)

Tessel Modules

The capabilities of a Tessel can be extended via "modules." On the Tessel 2, there are two module headers that provide pins to communicate with external devices. With modules, you can add the circuits and components needed to control motors or sensors. You can also build your own modules (*https://tessel.io/docs/DIYModule*)—for example, with help of Eagle or Kicad software packages. Figure 7-9, shows a simple diagram of an Eagle device for the Tessel module format.

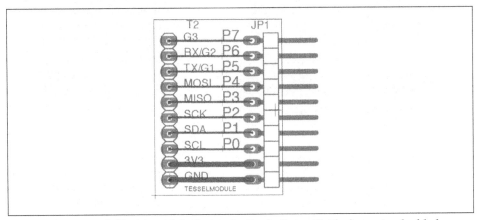

Figure 7-9. A simple Tessel module design for Eagle (https://github.com/embeddedno dejs/tessellib)

Different Tessel modules will be shown in later chapters. For now, you can observe that the ports of a Tessel are meant to easily control external components. The module header pins can communicate with sensors or actuators, for example.

Basic Components

Now that you know about different ways to connect circuits and multiple components, let's look closer at particular types of components. Components can be "passive" or "active."

Passive components are somewhat similar to mechanical parts like heatsinks, which mainly dissipate energy. Passive components such as resistors or potentiometers are often useful to generate reference voltages. In contrast, active components are used to power lights, sound, or motion.

Many components need some kind of driver software. In embedded projects with Node.js, you'll find many drivers for components at *http://npmjs.com*.

Still more concepts surrounding components influence the practice of writing software for hardware. We will review these additional concepts in the next section.

Datasheets

Electronic components are documented in datasheets. Typically, datasheets discuss the limits and constraints of device operation.

Most datasheets can be found online today. There are special search engines for datasheets, such as Parts.io (*http://parts.io*). Companies like SparkFun (*http://spark fun.com*) or Adafruit (*http://adafruit.com*) can help you to translate abstract datasheets into easy-to-understand information for components that they sell.

Key information you will find in a datasheet includes:

Operational voltage
> To protect your boards and other parts, it is often important to identify the operational voltage of components. For example, a Raspberry Pi works on 3.3V, and connecting a 5V pin of an Arduino might do some harm.

Communication with a part, such as what protocol it uses
> Simpler parts might output a digital signal or analog voltage. Others might specify PWM. On parts with their own microcontrollers, the datasheet will have details on the part's use of communication protocols such as I2C or SPI.

Symbols and footprint
> Schematics and footprints show how the various pins (e.g., the power and communication pins) need to be connected in order to function.

Passive Components

Many "passive" components are needed to adjust voltages or signal shapes. One simple passive component is the simple ceramic resistor, a physically static component made of ceramic and wire. In more advanced forms, passive components come as switches and potentiometers.

Potentiometers are often used to tune a voltage to a certain level. For example, a potentiometer can be used to adjust the volume of sound or the brightness of an LCD display. Another good use of a potentiometer is as an easy way to "simulate" a sensor. Sensors often output varying voltages. Turning the knob of a potentiometer that is connected to an analog pin often has a similar effect, but is easier to set up than the environment a sensor requires.

Besides providing voltage references, resistors and potentiometers also can protect active components such as an LED against high currents.

As shown in Figure 7-10, SparkFun provides a nice collection of passive and electromechanical components in the form of device libraries. A device library helps to organize components in a PCB project. The device libraries from SparkFun provide many useful prebuilt components. This includes electromechanical devices, such as tactile switches and trimming potentiometers.

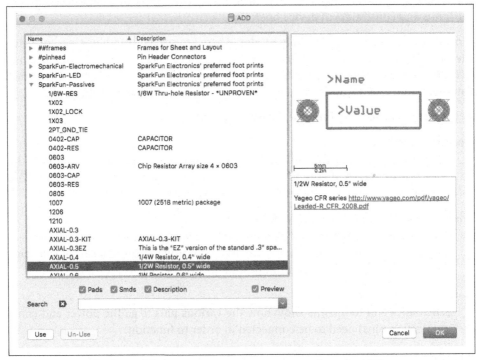

Figure 7-10. Eagle device library with passive components from SparkFun

LEDs

LEDs are simple "active" components because they convert electrical energy into light energy. In their earliest days, LEDs were used as simple outputs in displays, as shown in the Altair 8800 computer (Figure 7-11).

Figure 7-11. The Altair 8800 uses LEDs as a simple user display (source: https://flic.kr/p/ 5XrzTu)

In many embedded projects, LEDs are helpful to determine whether a device carries current or not. The LED datasheet shows two pins of an LED. The longer one (anode) is used for the positive voltage, while the shorter one (cathode) is used for the negative voltage. If the voltage difference between anode and cathode is above a certain level, the LED will emit light.

Different colors for LEDs usually have different operational voltages. This "forward voltage" at a certain operating current influences how brightly the LED shines. Depending on the operational voltage of your system, you can again calculate if and how much resistance you must apply to protect the LED.

Working with LEDs has many advantages: they are an easy way to visualize the working of a circuit and to check working software. You just have to apply a forward voltage and the LED will light up.

With a time-varying PWM signal, you also can modulate the brightness of an LED.

Sensors

Many embedded devices require inputs of some form. For example, in a weather station, you measure a physical property of the environment like temperature or humidity. This is done with sensors.

Data from sensors can be used to monitor and track processes, or to change an output of a device. The operation of a sensor is often visualized with a simple block, as shown in Figure 7-12.

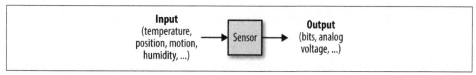

Figure 7-12. Voltages from a sensor measurement

Many different forms of sensors exist. One of the simplest examples is the temperature sensor. For devices that move, you can capture data about motion with gyroscopes or accelerometers. Also, measuring distance is easily possible with ultrasonic sound detectors.

Temperature

Measuring temperature is an easy start into physical computing. Temperature sensors also provide a nice "Hello, World!" experience when beginning with IoT development.

In Figure 7-13, you'll see two popular choices for capturing temperature. On the left is an approach used by the Grove Kit from Seeed Studio (*http://wiki.seeedstudio.com/wiki/Grove_-_Temperature_Sensor*), and on the right is a the DHT11 temperature and humidity sensor.

Figure 7-13. Two common forms for measuring temperature: a thermistor (left) and a DHT11 (right)

In the Grove Kit sensor, the temperature is mapped to a resistance. Combining this variable resistance with a known supply voltage, the temperature can be sampled with an analog input pin on a microcontroller. For Arduino users, you can find a sketch with a temperature sensor on the Seeed Studio Wiki page (*http://www.seeedstudio.com/wiki/Grove_-_Temperature_Sensor*).

In the case of a DHT11, the temperature is measured and encoded as a digital string of zeros and ones. The temperature can then be read with a digital pin. This sensor is especially popular with Arduino and Raspberry Pi.

Temperature sensors come in different accuracies and integration levels. If you need high accuracy, the MCP9808 is a popular choice that can be purchased on eBay. Also, the Atmel AT30TS750A that comes with the I2C Eduction Shield (see Figure 7-8) is easy to use.

Motion

Detecting motion can often be useful for robotics applications. A nice foundation for these kinds of projects is given by accelerometers, gyroscopes, and magnetometers. These components are often combined; for example, the SparkFun "9 Degrees of Freedom Board" uses the LSM9DS0 9DOF inertial measurement unit (IMU), as shown in Figure 7-14.

Another option to explore motion with an embedded device is the MPU6050. You will find a number of interesting examples online showing how to connect an Arduino to this component.

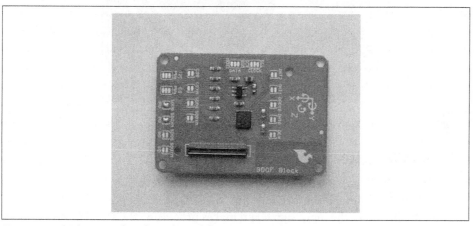

Figure 7-14. The IMU breakout board from SparkFun

 In the Embedded.fm podcast "Episode 9: Kidnapped and Blindfolded," Elicia White provides a nice overview of how these sensors work (*http://embedded.fm/episodes/2013/6/25/8-kidnapped-and-blindfolded*).

Another good option to experiment with motion is by purchasing a Nintendo Wii Nunchuk controller (shown in Figure 7-15) and attaching a breakout board to it. The Nunchuk gives you an accelerometer and a gyroscope in the plus version.

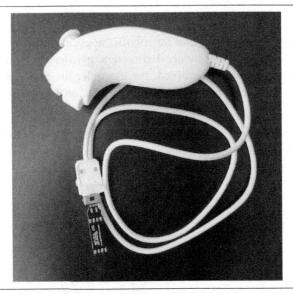

Figure 7-15. A Wii Nunchuk

Ultrasonic Distance

With ultrasonic distance sensors, you can easily add detection for obstacles to an embedded project. Several sensors exist but the SFR-10 is a popular one. The SFR-10 adds some filtering to the input signal and makes processing the signal easier.

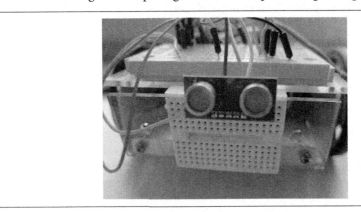

Figure 7-16. An SFR-10 mounted on a robot

Actuators

While sensors can capture data from physical phenomenon, actuators are used to drive motion or change things around you. A block diagram of an actuator is shown in Figure 7-17.

Speed or position of a motor are often controlled with "analog" output pins.

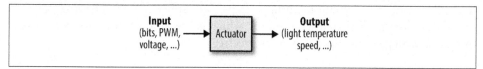

Figure 7-17. Voltage input to an actuator

The mapping from the "continuous" to the "discrete" world is done with ADCs, or "analog-to-digital" converters. The other direction is covered with DACs, "digital-to-analog" converters.

Servo Motors

Servo motors allow you to position something, such as pointers or steering wheels. They provide rotational motion in a limited range—imagine mapping a servo motor's range as a dial from zero to 100.

"Continuous" servo motors, so called because they do not have a limited range, are popular to turn cogs or wheels. Instead of setting position, on a continuous servo motor you can set the speed within a range, such as to control the speed of a vehicle.

Figure 7-18 shows a small servo motor. A servo motor has a gear box, a DC motor, and a rotor to move something. It typically has three wires: GND, power, and a reference signal.

Figure 7-18. A standard servo motor with three wires (in a ribbon cable)

The servo motor is contolled by an electric signal which measures the position of the rotor and determines the amount of movement based on feedback coming from the microcontroller.

Stepper Motors

Stepper motors are similar to servo motors in that they can be used to position something. The motor can rotate in certain "steps." A stepper motor is typically able to drive with more force than a servo motor, which is useful if you want to move something heavy. Stepper motors can be very precise.

DC Motors

DC motors leave much control to the engineer. Typically, they are used as power train for remote control vehicles. The speed of a motor is controlled by a voltage. The higher the voltage, the higher the current and the faster the motor rotates. However, building a feedback loop to accurately control speed or position with a DC motor is more difficult.

Multimedia

Special components are needed for multimedia applications, such as displays and cameras. Let's quickly review some options in that space.

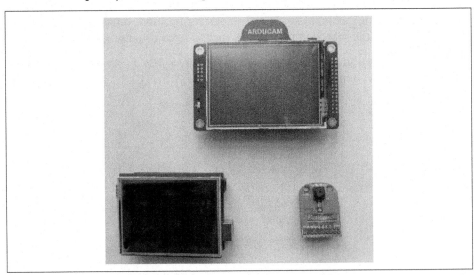

Figure 7-19. Outputs for multimedia

Displays come in many different technologies. For multimedia applications, LCD and TFT displays are especially interesting.

To drive many pixels on a display, you'll often require a special processor or a more powerful processor than a simple Arduino will have.

On an embedded Linux system, you'll need a display driver in the form of a frame-buffer such as *https://github.com/notro/fbtft*.

Cables

To make a connection between devices for debugging, providing power, or simply controlling devices, it is often necessary to work with multiple cables. USB cables in particular are widely used.

Jumper Wires

Generally if you work with hardware it is a good idea to build an inventory of different kinds of jumper wires. There are male-to-female wires, male-to-male wires, and female-to-female wires.

USB Cables

Working with embedded devices, it is often a good idea to gather a number of USB cables with different plug types.

The USB Micro B type is slowly becoming a default for programming microcontroller boards. Yet, you'll also encounter boards and setups where you require USB Mini or type A cables.

FTDI-USB-Cable

Most microcontroller boards have a serial port that can be used for debugging signals. Sometimes, direct access to the serial port of a processor is the only way to see output when debugging firmware.

To make working with serial ports for development easier, it is often a good idea to build or buy an adapter cable to use on a serial port.

Network Cables

The last type of cable that is useful when developing IoT devices are classic network cables. Network cables in combination with USB-to-Ethernet adapters are also useful to share Internet connections.

## CHAPTER 8

Node.js Libraries for Hardware

In this chapter, we'll continue programming hardware with JavaScript. By now, you have made some basic steps to set up hardware and a software toolchain. Let's go beyond the blinking LED. This chapter begins by introducing a library to communicate with an embedded device over a serial port.

Next, after sending and reading bytes from a device, it is time to look into representations of components in JavaScript. For this, the library Johnny-Five will get you going.

Finally, this chapter closes with some ideas and instructions on using your new knowledge to experiment in a variety of directions.

Most examples will still work with a simple Arduino Uno. But with a board that supports embedded Linux, you can run the examples inside an embedded device too. As for components, the Seeed Studio Grove Kit should cover most of the examples for now. The Grove Kit shield lets you quickly connect components such as buttons and outputs to your base board.

 The Johnny-Five Inventor's Kit includes a set of hardware with tutorials that explain how to use Tessel 2 with Johnny-Five. You can see some experiments using Johnny-Five on the Tessel 2 (and associated hardware kit) in the "Experiment Guide for the Johnny-Five Inventor's Kit" (*https://learn.sparkfun.com/tutorials/experiment-guide-for-the-johnny-five-inventors-kit/introduction-to-the-johnny-five-inventors-kit*).

You'll also see some examples that are based on the LibMRAA library. Don't be confused by its name—it does not (yet) have a meaning. What's important is that this library provides bindings for JavaScript to low-level pin functions and interrupts.

JavaScript for the Hardware Abstraction Layer

The language of circuits consists of signals, voltages, currents, and pins. Program pins and signals are fundamental in embedded development. However, after a certain point, you must translate the hardware into the language of software. Embedded engineers call this interface between hardware and software the *hardware abstraction layer* (HAL).

The HAL hides details of components and peripherals and helps to make software libraries compatible with different kinds of hardware. For example, you can run the same Arduino code on different boards, such as an Arduino Uno or Arduino Nano.

As JavaScript is a high-level language, you can find many interesting objects and libraries to make hardware abstractions. In an IoT project, you want to manage different hardware "resources" at different abstraction levels (see Figure 8-1). On the outer level, there might be a board object. On a board, there are pin objects that deal with analog or digital signals. Attached to a pin, there might be components such as an LED object that you want to control.

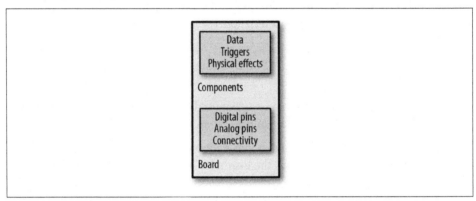

Figure 8-1. Basic categories for hardware abstractions

Within the Node Package Manager (npm), there are many JavaScript libraries to translate buttons or signals for communication into JavaScript objects. Exploring the forms of JavaScript objects for hardware is the goal of this chapter. In later chapters, you will see how to combine JavaScript libraries for hardware with services and the Internet.

Good hardware abstraction layers are formulated in these JavaScript libraries:

serialport
> The node-serialport library provides some simple JavaScript objects for communication between devices. With this library you obtain a data stream to read and

---

write bytes to the serial port. Experimenting with serial communication will give you insight into general communication problems.

Johnny-Five

This project by Rick Waldron has been around since 2012 and pioneered a number of ideas for JavaScript hardware development. Johnny-Five runs on many boards, including Arduino, Tessel, Intel Edison, and Raspberry Pi. In addition to boards, the library provides a number of nice abstractions for hardware components such as LEDs, switches, and accelerometers.

Cylon.js

This project by Ron Evans has been around since 2013 and provides a hardware abstraction layer for different IoT devices.

MRAA

LibMRAA provides a bridge between low-level driver software for components for Intel boards mainly. With LibMRAA, you get a bridge from JavaScript to lower-level programming languages that are needed for embedded development.

We'll first look at some examples of JavaScript abstractions for serial communication. After that, you'll see some examples based on the Johnny-Five library. Johnny-Five also supports a so-called read-eval-print-loop (REPL) that makes it easy explore and play with components.

---

npm Commands

npm is a core utility when writing a Node.js application. Here are the main commands:

`npm init`
Creates a new manifest file package.json. In this file, you can store meta information on a project as well as the dependency list.

`npm install`
The first command you run whenever you clone a Node.js project.

`npm install --save`
Adds libraries to an empty project, e.g., `npm install --save johnny-five`.

`npm config set proxy`
Configures npm to use a proxy on an intranet.

`npm run start`
Runs scripts. This shortcut must be defined in the package.json.

The node-serialport Library

When you work with embedded devices, you'll often find yourself in a situation where you must transfer data from one device to another. In its simplest form, this means providing a cable link such as a RS-232 or USB cable between two devices, as shown in Figure 8-2.

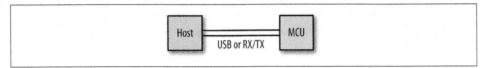

Figure 8-2. A serial link between devices

With the JavaScript library for serial communication, you obtain some objects and functions to send data from one device to another. The node-serialport library was authored by Chris Williams. Many hardware projects employ serial communication in one way or another. Before exploring the library, let's quickly provide an overview of use cases and concepts.

Serial Communication with JavaScript

Why would JavaScript for serial communication be more interesting than using another programming language? The CodeBender platform offers a good example. As shown in Figure 8-3, the website allows you to flash your Arduino directly from the browser. While the embedded code is built on the server, the code is uploaded to the devices via the browser and a USB cable. Behind the scenes is serial communication with JavaScript at work.

After you flash your Arduino with the example code shown here, you can monitor the value of a sensor in the serial console of the browser. This example is an excellent demonstration of serial communication.

Have a look at Figure 8-4. In general, serial communication is based on the following idea: a transmitter (TX) has one line to send data and a receiver (RX) has another line to receive data. Two wires allow you to send and receive data independently from each other, which is called *full-duplex* communication.

Because TX and RX are hard-wired signals between devices, the communication protocol can be kept simple. By defining a data rate beforehand, a clock signal is not necessary. When you want to have more flexible communication, you can share a clock signal to share timing information between transmitter and receiver.

Figure 8-3. The CodeBender platform links an Arduino to a web browser with serial communication

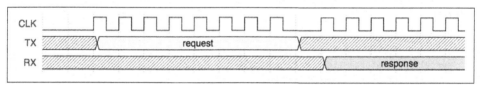

Figure 8-4. Serial communication provides a protocol to transfer data between devices

The core building block of a serial port is a *universal asynchronous receiver and transmitter* (UART). Some datasheets refer to ports that are based on a *universal synchronous/asynchronous receiver and transmitter* (USART). In the case of a UART, clock information is automatically recovered from the incoming data stream, which simplifies the configuration of a port somewhat, while a USART can be driven by an external clock signal allowing for much faster transmission speeds and support for a variety of protocols.

If you are interested in learning more about hardware communication protocols, Kevin Sidwar and Kelsey Breseman's blog post "A Web Developer's Guide to Communication Protocols" (*https:// tessel.io/blog/108840925797/a-web-developers-guide-to- communication-protocols*) provides a good introduction to several, including how they work and why you might choose them.

On a host computer, an operating system connects to the UART via a software driver. The driver takes care of inputs and outputs and configuration of the signals ("I/O control," or `ioctl` in embedded language). This means if you want to talk to an Arduino from your laptop with Node.js, your JavaScript will actually talk to the driver for the serial port of the operating system.

With these concepts, you are ready to explore the node-serialport library. First, we will discuss how to scan for devices with JavaScript. Then, once you can find your device, the next step is to receive data, or to "dump" data coming from a device. Finally, you will learn how to send data from JavaScript to a device.

Scanning for Devices

To get started with the serialport library, let's first create a fresh JavaScript project and add this module to it:

```
$ npm install --save-dev serialport
```

After the module has been downloaded, you are ready to start some serial communication fun:

```
// list_ports.js
var serialPort = require("serialport");
serialPort.list(function (err, ports) {
  ports.forEach(function(port) {
    console.log(port.comName);
  });
});
```

Now connect an Arduino with a USB cable to your computer. After the devices are connected, run:

```
$ node list_ports.js
```

You should see something similar to:

```
$ node list_ports.js
/dev/cu.Bluetooth-Incoming-Port |
/dev/cu.Bluetooth-Modem |
/dev/cu.usbmodem1411 | Arduino (www.arduino.cc)
```

In this case, there is an Arduino connected at */dev/cu.usbmodem1411*. Because listing connected devices at the serial port is a useful command, you can add a shortcut in the *package.json* to extend npm with new features:

```
"scripts": {
  "list_ports": "node list_ports.js"
}
```

You can now run the following npm command:

```
$ npm run list_ports

> ch08@1.0.0 list_ports
> node list_ports.js

/dev/cu.Bluetooth-Incoming-Port |
/dev/cu.Bluetooth-Modem |
/dev/cu.usbmodem1411 | Arduino (www.arduino.cc)
```

Receiving Data from Arduino

Now that you can list devices that are attached on a serial port, let's capture some data from a device. You must pass the port name, something like *COM1* on Windows or */dev/ttyS0* on POSIX platforms. In the example above, the Arduino is on port */dev/cu.usbmodem1411*.

Let's prepare an Arduino to send some data over to your host computer. Instead of using a sensor, let's use *counter.ino*, a simpler Arduino sketch that simply increases a counter (you'll see how to capture that data with Node.js momentarily):

```
// Arduino sketch for testing serial communication
setup() {
  Serial.begin(9600);
}

int i=0;
void loop() {
  Serial.println(i++);
  delay(100); // poll every 100ms
}
```

The last "delay" gives the laptop some time to process the data. Providing a delay is a good idea when you want to watch a data stream with human eyes instead of a CPU's.

 When you configure a serial port, you must sometimes include things such as flow control, parity, stop bits, and character size, but this is out of scope for most Arduino projects.

For Arduino projects, a good choice for transmission speed is 9600 baud, because it is slow enough to watch incoming bits "live." If there is a speed mismatch between your computer and your Arduino, you'll see garbled output.

To read bits from the port with JavaScript, you must first open the port:

```
// read_port.js
var serialport = require("serialport");
var SerialPort = serialport.SerialPort;

var serialPort = new SerialPort("/dev/cu.usbmodem14131", {
  baudrate: 9600,
  parser: serialport.parsers.readline("\n")
});

serialPort.on("open", function () {
  // capture data
});
```

When the serial port is instantiated (as var serialPort = new SerialPort), the final argument sets a parser for the incoming data. In this example, we use the default readline parser, which yields human-readable text broken up by newlines.

Once the serial port is open, you have access to its data stream. The easiest thing to do is dump data from the stream to the terminal:

```
// read_port.js
var serialport = require("serialport");
var SerialPort = serialport.SerialPort;

var serialPort = new SerialPort("/dev/cu.usbmodem14131", {
  baudrate: 9600,
  parser: serialport.parsers.readline("\n")
});

serialPort.on("open", function () {
  console.log('open');
  serialPort.on('data', function(data) {
    console.log(data);
  });
});
```

As you can see, the serialPort object listens to the data events from the port. The received bits are displayed to the screen with console.log(data).

If everything works out, you'll see some numbers from the Arduino scrolling down on the screen. By adding some components, you can easily dump data from measurements (e.g., temperature or positions from a potentiometer).

Sending Data to Arduino

Let's now look at sending data to an embedded device—for example, simple control commands.

To see how this works, let's write a very basic command parser (*https://www.ardu ino.cc/en/Reference/ParseInt*) for an Arduino board:

```
// Arduino sketch to test receiving data
if (Serial.available() > 0) {
  incoming = Serial.parseInt();

  if (Serial.read() == '\n') {
    // light the display
  }
}
```

With this code, the Arduino examines its UART to determine whether there is data in the receive buffer. If so, the Arduino parses the data and does something, such as toggling LEDs. To see some options, have a look in the ReadASCIIString example or the parseInt API in the Arduino documentation.

On the JavaScript side, you can define a "write" callback to write to the serial port. When you include the serial port in the previous example, the code becomes:

```
// write_data.js
var Stream = require('stream');

var modem = 'cu.usbmodem14231';

var ws = new Stream();
ws.writable = true;

ws.write = function(data) {
  serialPort.write(data);
};

ws.end = function(buf) {
  console.log('bye');
}

var serialPort = new SerialPort('/dev/' + modem, {
  baudrate: 9600,
  parser: serialport.parsers.readline("\n")
});

process.stdin.pipe(ws);
```

The idea behind this JavaScript code is that you redirect the output from, for example, the computer console into a writable stream. Data from this stream is then written into the serial port with serialPort.write(data).

If you want to learn about C++ integration to JavaScript, studying the node-serialport library is a good start. The serialport library currently uses the Node Native Addons (nan.js). This approach supports multiple platforms to integrate JavaScript with C++.

The Johnny-Five Library

Johnny-Five comes with many JavaScript classes for components to work with.[1] Instead of translating desired behavior to the technical workings of a board pin, you can directly use a button or LED class that provides a default behavior.

An Empty Project

To begin, you need an empty project from which you can install JavaScript dependencies.

On your host machine, let's create an empty project with:

```
$ mkdir led13
```

Next, you can use the npm to initialize the project:

```
$ npm init -y
```

The first dependency to install is Johnny-Five.

This library includes plugins for various boards including Intel Galileo and Edison boards. You can install Johnny-Five as follows:

```
$ npm install --save johnny-five
```

As you can see in the directory, you now have a file called *package.json*. This is the project manifest, where you can add different dependencies.

Depending on the board you are working with, you must use a board "adapter." For example, in the case of the Intel Edison, this means:

```
$ npm install --save edison-io
```

With these libraries, you are ready to go.

The Board Object

The core class of a Johnny-Five project is the board class. In its simplest form (connecting to an Arduino Uno), the board is initialized as follows:

---

1 Johnny-Five was a fictional robot character in the movie Short Circuit (1986) (*http://www.imdb.com/title/tt0091949*). He was an experimental robot who was struck by lightning, became intelligent, and escaped from a lab.

```
// board_ready.js
var five = require("johnny-five");
var board = new five.Board();
```

The script will search for an Arduino connected to the host computer. To specify the serial port where the board is connected, you can add a parameter port as follows:

```
var board = new five.Board({
  port: '/dev/cu.usbmodem12'
});
```

Johnny-Five supports many different boards. For example, if you want to control an Intel Edison with Johnny-Five, you pass the Edison board adapter when you set up the board:

```
var edison = require('edison-io');

var board = new five.Board({
  io: new Edison()
});
```

Once you have a board instance, you can easily capture events from a board object. For example, the board will emit a "ready" event that you can capture like this:

```
board.on("ready", function() {
  console.log("Board is ready!");
});
```

The fun really starts with objects inside the "ready" callback.

The Johnny-Five REPL

As a first experiment with hardware, let's set up the read-eval-print-loop (REPL). Similar to working with a console or terminal, a REPL gives you the chance to interactively inspect a hardware setup. It's like having a command line for your hardware.

You can also inject variables into an interactive programming session with:

```
// simple_repl.js
var five = require("johnny-five");

var Edison = require("edison-io");
var board = new five.Board({
  io: new Edison()
});

board.on("ready", function() {
  console.log("Board is ready!");

  this.repl.inject({
    led13: new five.Led(led13)
  });
});
```

The LED13 is now available in the console once you run this script with:

```
$ node simple_repl.js
```

We can then do some simple tests in the Node REPL:

```
>> led13.low();
>> led13.high();
```

Now that we have a working system with a blinking LED, let's look at capturing user input.

Buttons

The simplest way to capture user input is with buttons. Johnny-Five makes working with buttons very easy, as you can simply "subscribe" to events from a button. The events a button can emit are "down," "up," and "hold." To see how this works, let's look at the following example:

```
// button_tests.js

// import dependencies
var five = require("johnny-five");
var Edison = require("edison-io");
var board = new five.Board({
  io: new Edison()
});

var button, oe;

// init board
board.on("ready", function() {

button = new five.Button(7);
button.on('down', function() {
  console.log('button down');
});

button.on('up', function() {
  console.log('button up');
});

button.on('hold', function() {
  console.log('button hold');
});

  // provide variables for interactive session
  this.repl.inject({
button: button
  });
});
```

With these simple events, you could build a simple stopwatch—the first button press starts the clock, the second press stops the clock, and a "hold" event resets the clock.

Analog Inputs

A user can easily change the state of a device with a button press. In an application, you might need analog inputs instead of digital buttons. In contrast to a digital input such as a button, an analog input is more like a measurement.

With Johnny-Five, you can directly read data from an "analog" component such as a potentiometer, slider, or sensor.

Let's take a look at how to do this:

```
// read_analog.js

var five = require('johnny-five');
var Edison = require('edison-io');

var board = new five.Board({
  io: new Edison()
});

board.on("ready", function() {

var slider = new five.Sensor("A0");

  // "slide" is an alias for "change"
  slider.scale([0, 100]).on("slide", function() {
    console.log("slide", this.value);
  });
});
```

There are two differences between working with an analog input and working with a button: first, you provide a scale for the input, and second, you listen for "change" events and do something with its value.

Another example for analog inputs is reading data from sensors. Or, to read data from a whole lot of sensors such as the Nintendo Wii Nunchuk.

Proximity

If you want to build a robot, one common approach for obstacle detection is an ultrasonic distance meter. Johnny-Five has a nice module to work with proximity detectors.

Look at the following code for an example based on the SRF10 sensor:

```
// check_proximity.js

var five = require("johnny-five");
```

```
var board = new five.Board();

board.on("ready", function() {
  var proximity = new five.Proximity({
    controller: "SRF10"
  });

proximity.on("data", function() {
  console.log(this.cm + "cm", this.in + "in");
});

  proximity.on("change", function() {
    console.log("The obstruction has moved.");
  });
});
```

Nodebot

Johnny-Five was built for robots. Thanks to the `Nodebot` class, you can program a simple robot with only 12 lines of code:

```
// simple_nodebot.js
var five, Nodebot;

five = require("johnny-five");

five.Board().on("ready", function() {
  Nodebot = new five.Nodebot({
    right: 10,
    left: 11
  });

  this.repl.inject({
    n: Nodebot
  });
})
```

When you start this program, you'll have a REPL from which you can control the robot. In this case, the robot has two servo motors for a moving robot. If you want to test this out with a serial cable, it can be handy to mount the robot in a position in which it does not move.

We will learn more about building robots in Chapter 12.

The I2C Library

Compared to serial communication via UART, communication via I2C is a bit more complex. Many sensors and electronic components support I2C because it supports many sensors on the same bus using only two wires.

The I2C bus is a *half-duplex* interface, which means two nodes (usually called "master" and "slave") can only communicate over the wires *in turn*. When one node is listening, the other node can talk and vice versa. Imagine a phone call where only one party is allowed to speak and the other one must listen.

In I2C communication, the data line for communication is called SDA. The I2C bus adds another wire for providing timing information. The two wires, SDA (data) and SCL (clock), are both bidirectional.

The I2C specification version 3.0 defines four speed categories: Standard mode at up to 100 kbits/s, Fast mode at up to 400 kbits/s, Fast mode Plus at up to 1 Mbits/s, and High Speed mode at up to 3.4 Mbits/s.

There are different Node.js I2C libraries for I2C, for example using `sysfs`.

The LibMRAA Library

The MRAA library offers a number of interesting bindings to hardware. Originally, MRAA was an open source library for Intel Galileo and Edison boards, and supports an API similar to Arduino for different high-level programming languages. The library provides low-level access to GPIOs, PWM, and analog I/O ports.

MRAA Setup

MRAA is based on C++ libraries that access the operating system on a low level. This means that to use MRAA from JavaScript, you must install some C libraries first.

On an Intel Edison, this means adding `libmraa` dependencies to the board first:

```
echo "src mraa-upm http://iotdk.intel.com/repos/1.1/intelgalactic" >
  /etc/opkg/mraa-upm.conf
opkg update
opkg install libmraa0
```

With this, you can install the Node.js bindings to `libmraa` with:

```
npm install --save mraa
```

Let's check that it worked by creating a file called *hello.js*:

```
// hello.js
var mraa = require('mraa');
console.log('MRAA Version: ' + mraa.getVersion());
```

If everything worked, you should see:

```
# node hello.js
MRAA Version: v0.8.0
```

Let's look next at processing inputs and outputs with MRAA.

Outputs

Similar to Arduino, libmraa provides different output modes for pins.

As usual, digital outputs provide a good start for exploring a setup. In MRAA, a digital output can take a state 0 or 1:

```
// simple_blink.js
var mraa=require('mraa');

var led = new mraa.Gpio(8);
led.dir(mraa.DIR_OUT);
```

With led.dir(mraa.DIR_OUT) you specify the direction of a GPIO. In this case, it acts as an output. Then you could use the event loop in JavaScript to write 0 and 1 to the pin as follows:

```
var blink = 0;
setInterval(function() {
  blink = !blink;
  blink ? led.write(1) : led.write(0);
}, 2000);
```

In this example, the timeout is 2000 milliseconds (2 seconds).

You can also generate PWM signals (because the PWM signal is generated by the Linux operating system, the granularity of the PWM is a bit lower than on a microcontroller):

```
// hello_pwm.js
var pin = new mraa.Pwm(3);
pin.period(200);
pin.enable(true);

var level = 0;
setInterval(function() {
  pin.write(level);
  level+=0.01;
  if (level >= 1) {
    level = 0;
  }
}, 50);
```

This concludes our introduction to pins as outputs. Let's take a look at input pins.

Reading Inputs

To use a pin as digital input, you must declare the direction of the pin first:

```
// simple_buttons.js
var button = new mraa.Gpio(4);
button.dir(mraa.DIR_IN);
```

Next, you can read the state of the pin with:

```
setInterval(function() {
  var input = button.read();
  console.log(input);
}, 200);
```

To read an analog input, you'll address the pin with:

```
var analogPin0 = new mraa.Aio(0);
```

Now you can fetch the data with:

```
setInterval(function() {
  var sample = analogPin0.read();
  var sampleFloat = analogPin0.readFloat();
  console.log(sample);
  console.log(sampleFloat);
}, 300);
```

As you can see, the pin abstractions from MRAA are very low-level. To prevent re-writing drivers for sensors and components from scratch, you can load JavaScript drivers for MRAA projects with the UPM project. UPM stands for "useful packages and modules," and a number of drivers exist already, such as *https://www.npmjs.com/package/jsupm_joystick12*.

Interrupts

In contrast to other JavaScript libraries, LibMRAA allows you to bind functions to external interrupts from pins. This means you can avoid "blocking" code to detect pin changes and jump to code directly when it is needed.

The following example shows the usage of an interrupt on a GPIO pin:

```
// interrupt_check.js
var mraa = require('mraa');

function h() {
  console.log('button press');
}

var pin = new mraa.Gpio(4);
pin.isr(mraa.EDGE_FALLING, h);

setInterval(function() {
  console.log("nothing happened");
}, 400);
```

On the hardware side, you can add a button to digital pin 4 of a Galileo or Edison. If you then run the code:

```
$ node isr_example.js
```

You should see something like:

```
nothing happened
nothing happened
button press
nothing happened
```

As soon as GPIO 4 goes down, the interrupt is triggered. In this case, the callback function is executed.

Communications

LibMRAA also provides a number of low-level libraries for communication with other hardware devices. For example, to communicate with I2C:

```
var x = new mraa.I2c(0);
x.address(0x62);
x.writeReg(0, 0);
```

This can be tested with a simple I2C memory, for example.

For UART, you can use the following code:

```
u.setBaudRate(115200);
u.setMode(8, 0, 1);
u.setFlowcontrol(false, false);
u.writeStr("test\n");
```

The Cylon.js Library

The Cylon.js library by Ron Evans and Adrian Zankich aims to bring the ease of jQuery to IoT applications. The library brings an object-oriented approach to working with hardware devices and aims to make robotics applications portable across platforms. The library comes with good documentation and provides some help on board setup for JavaScript too.

To see how the library works, let's look at the following code example:

```
// cylon_blink.js
var Cylon = require('cylon');

Cylon.robot({
  connections: {
    galileo: { adaptor: 'intel-iot' }
  },
  devices: {
    led: { driver: 'led', pin: 13},
    button: { driver: 'button', pin: 8}
  },
  work: function(my) {
    my.button.on('push', function() {
      my.led.toggle();
```

```
    });
  }
}).start();
```

With `Cylon.robot()`, you instantiate a new "robot" object. The configuration of a robot is based on a number of properties: connections, devices, and a `work` function.

In this example, the robot is connected to an Intel Galileo board. With only one change in variable, this code can be run on different boards such as a BeagleBone or Arduino.

Next, you can add devices that the robots should control. Note that there is a `driver` property that provides the necessary hardware abstraction layer.

Last, there is the `work` function, where you can program how the robot controls devices. In this case, a button toggles an LED.

## CHAPTER 9

Exploring Network Protocols

Network protocols are an important piece of a connected system. Network protocols define rules about how devices at different locations should communicate.

Using a weather station as an example, we will discuss different roles that devices can play in a network. The Hypertext Transfer Protocol (HTTP) is based on requests and responses.[1] When a weather display requests information from a server, the embedded device acts as client. When an embedded device provides weather data, it can act as server. Sometimes, a device can be both client and server.

While HTTP is stateless, other network protocols support maintaining "connections" between devices. For example, with the transmission control protocol (TCP) or websockets, transmissions of data packets can happen without prior requests. The Web-Socket protocol is particularly popular for pushing data to a web browser—for example, whenever new data is available.

In the Node.js ecosystem, there are libraries to work with all kinds of network protocols. Support for HTTP and TCP comes in the form of Node.js core modules. For the WebSocket protocol, you can fetch open source libraries via npm.

Another important network protocol is the MQTT protocol, which is used to send messages across networks. MQTT will be discussed in Chapter 11 in the context of cloud services for connected devices.

---

1 A variant of HTTP for IoT projects is CoAP (*https://tools.ietf.org/html/rfc7252*). Most examples for HTTP should translate to CoAP with some efforts.

The Hypertext Transfer Protocol

HTTP describes the transfer of state between client and server. HTTP is one of the pillars behind the World Wide Web. With HTTP, an embedded device can answer requests from other places in a network, or it can itself send updates or fetch instructions from a server.

Requesting the Weather

Due to their simplicity, weather displays and stations offer an easy-to-understand illustration of the usage of requests and responses of HTTP with embedded devices. On the hardware side, you could build a simple weather display with Grove components (discussed in Chapter 7). Another option would be to buy a small display and temperature/humidity sensors from eBay, SparkFun, or Adafruit and solder them together.

Gathering the components for a weather display might take some time. In the meantime, you can study its functions by looking at the weather app on your smartphone first. What happens if you request the weather for a certain location?

As you can see on the left side of Figure 9-1, your smartphone acts as a user agent that requests weather data from a public weather database. The smartphone is an "output" device that consists of a display and a network connection.

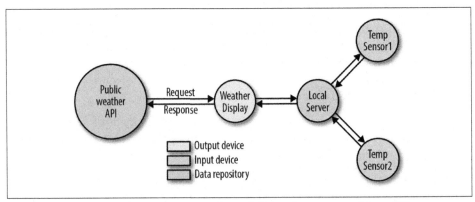

Figure 9-1. Weather information comes from different locations and has different outputs (displays) and inputs (sensors)

By adding "input" devices with sensors, you could connect your own weather stations to a weather display. This is shown on the right side of Figure 9-1.

Input and output devices do not translate directly to requests and responses of HTTP. According to RFC2616 (*http://www.w3.org/Protocols/rfc2616/rfc2616-sec6.html*), responses provide a status code and an information body. It is this information body that should be processed and rendered on the display.

JavaScript allows you to prototype a weather display in a web browser, on the command line, and on the embedded devices. Instead of a web browser, the Node.js script acts as "user agent." The script requests the weather station on behalf of the user. Different weather displays can fetch weather data from the same (public) database as shown in Figure 9-2.

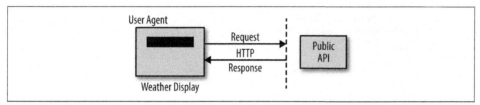

Figure 9-2. Clients for weather data and weather stations

There are different public databases that provide weather data. And at npm you will find different modules to work with weather data. A good option is weather-js (*https://www.npmjs.com/package/weather-js*).

In a new directory, you first initialize the project and install the module with:

```
$ npm init -y
$ npm install weather-js
```

Next, you can set up a script to fetch the weather data from the MSN weather forecast service:

```
// hello_weather.js
var weather = require('weather-js');
var location = 'Paris, France';
var degreeType = 'C';

weather.find({search: location, degreeType: degreeType}, function(err, result) {
  if (err) {
      console.log(err);
      process.exit(0);
  }
  console.log(result);
});
```

Behind the scenes, the Node.js modules request and xml2js make an HTTP request and provide the response as a JSON object. Before attaching an embedded device to interact with the weather, let's quickly check that the API works from the command line.

If you run:

```
$ node hello_weather.js
```

You'll see:

```
current:
 { temperature: '10',
   skycode: '31',
   skytext: 'Clear',
   date: '2016-03-27',
   observationtime: '22:00:00',
   observationpoint: 'Paris, Paris, France',
   feelslike: '7',
   humidity: '66',
   winddisplay: '28 km/h South',
   day: 'Sunday',
   shortday: 'Sun',
   windspeed: '28 km/h',
   imageUrl: 'http://blob.weather.microsoft.com/static/weather4/en-us/law/31.gif' },
 forecast: ...
```

The next step is to allow users of an embedded device to fetch weather data with the press of a button. Instead of the computer console, we want to display the result to an output (i.e., a screen).

Putting together hardware for a weather display with an Arduino can be as simple as the setup shown in Figure 9-3. You can connect a button to D4 on a Grove shield and an LCD display to the I2C bus.

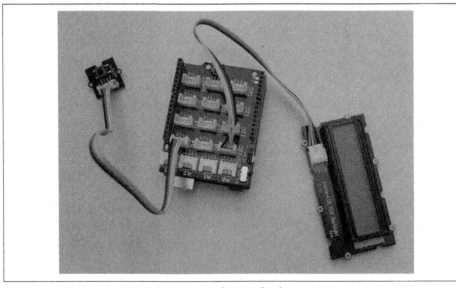

Figure 9-3. Arduino with push button and LCD display

Programming the screen on a button press is similar to the examples from the previous chapters. With the Johnny-Five library, it looks like this:

```
$ npm install --save johnny-five
```

Then, capture a button press as follows:

```
// weather_display.js
var five = require('johnny-five');
var board = new five.Board();

board.on('ready', function() {

var button = new five.Button(4);

// To display weather information
var lcd = new five.LCD({
  controller: "JHD1313M1"
});

  // Update screen on button press
  button.on('press', function() {
    console.log('press');
    lcd.clear();
    lcd.print("hello");
  });
});
```

Last, you can add the *hello_weather.js* script to the Johnny-Five Arduino wrapper:

```
// weather_display.js
var weather = require('weather-js');
var location = 'Paris, France';
var degreeType = 'C';

var five = require('johnny-five');
var board = new five.Board();

board.on('ready', function() {
    var button = new five.Button(4);
    var lcd = new five.LCD({
        controller: "JHD1313M1"
    });

// on press, fetch the weather
    button.on('press', function() {
        lcd.clear();
        weather.find({search: location, degreeType: degreeType},
                    function(err, result) {
            if (err) {
                console.log("problem fetching weather");
                console.log(err);
                process.exit(0);
```

```
        }
      lcd.cursor(0,0).print(location);
      lcd.cursor(1,0).print("temp: "+ result[0].current.temperature);
    });
  });
});
```

If successful, you'll see the temperature of the requested place on the LCD.

Prepare the HTTP Client

Before building your own HTTP server that acts as a weather station, it is a good idea to prepare an API client for testing. As shown in Figure 9-4, an API client handles GET requests to fetch state, and POST requests to update state.

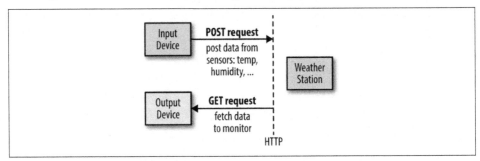

Figure 9-4. Different usages for POST and GET requests

On npmjs.com, you'll find many libraries that help you write custom HTTP clients. The most popular are request (*https://www.npmjs.com/package/request*) and super-agent (*https://www.npmjs.com/package/superagent*). We'll use request as it is one of the most popular Node.js modules.

In a new project, install the request module with:

```
$ npm install --save request
```

A get request allows you to fetch data via a *uniform resource locator* (URL).

To have a script act as a user agent:

```
// get_request.js
var request=require('request');

// take url from command line
var url=process.argv[2];
if (!url) {
  console.log('You must add a path.');
}
console.log('GET url: ' + url);

var headers = {'User-Agent': 'Sensor Agent'};
```

```
request.get(url, {headers: headers})
        .on('error', function(err) {
            console.log(err)
    }).pipe(process.stdout);
```

On Linux systems, you can make the code executable with the hash-bang syntax. In front of the script, you can add:

```
#!/usr/bin/env node
```

Now to test this agent, let's query data from the book website:

```
$ ./simple_agent.js http://embeddednodejs.com/dummy_data.json
GET url: http://embeddednodejs.com/dummy_data.json
[{"time":"00:00", "data": 0}, {"time":"11:11", "data": 1}]
```

Similarly, you can invoke POST and PUT requests:

```
// post_request
var request=require('request');

// the URL for the weather station to come
var url = "http://localhost:4000/measurements";

var headers = {'User-Agent': 'Sensor Agent',
               'content-type': 'application/json'};
var data = {temp: 25};
request({url: url,
         method: 'POST',
         form: data,
         headers: headers})
        .on('error', function(err) {
            console.log(err)
        }).pipe(process.stdout);
```

You can automate running scripts to fetch or post data with forever:

```
$ forever start -o log.txt --spinSleepTime 1000 get_request.js

$ npm install -g forever
```

Building a Weather Station

A weather station should manage weather data from multiple sensor devices. For this, it must deal with a couple of paths or HTTP routes to manage measurements at a weather station, as illustrated in Figure 9-5. To store data, the server must process POST requests from a sensor device. To display data, the server should response to GET requests.

Let's start by creating a web server locally on your laptop. Later, you can transfer the web server to a device with embedded Linux.

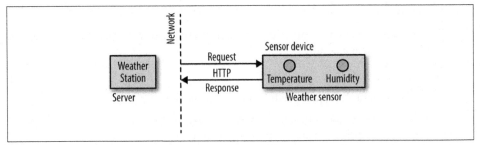

Figure 9-5. A weather station can process requests from sensor devices

You can set up a file *weather_server.js* as follows:

```javascript
// weather_server.js
var express = require('express'); // to create a server
var morgan = require('morgan'); // to log HTTP requests
var bodyParser = require('body-parser'); // to process incoming POST requests

var port = 4000;

// create server
var app = express();
app.use(morgan('combined'));
app.use(bodyParser.urlencoded({ extended: false }));

// basic routes
app.get('/', function(req, res) {
   res.writeHead(200);
   res.write('weather station is up');
   res.end();
});

// measurements
app.get('/measurements/:measurement_id', function(req, res) {
   res.writeHead(200);
   res.write('data from measurement');
   res.end();
});

app.post('/measurements', function(req, res) {
   console.log('temp is: ' + req.body.temp);
   res.writeHead(200);
   res.write('storing data.');
   res.end();
});

var server = app.listen(port);
```

The first thing we do is create a server. In this example, the Express.js (*http://expressjs.com*) framework is used. To log HTTP requests, the middleware `morgan` is used. To process data from incoming POST requests, the middleware `bodyParser` is added as well.

 There are plenty of server frameworks that can help you automate the basic setup of a server, including Hapi.js and Meteor. For a nice overview of web servers, check out "Node.js Frameworks: The 10 Best for Web and Apps Development" (*http://noeticforce.com/best-nodejs-frameworks-for-web-and-app-development*).

After the middleware, a number of routes for HTTP requests are added—for example, requests to receive information about a measurement and requests to process POST requests from sensor agents.

Note that the `req` and `res` objects of the route callbacks are called *streams*. This means that to build a response, you write `res.write()`. To end the processing, you need to close the request with `res.end()` to transport the response back to the client.

To see this server in action, you must start the server with:

```
$ node weather_station
```

Then you can navigate your browser to `localhost:4000`. Or, you can send a request with the user agent from the previous section:

```
$ node get_measurements
[]
```

An empty response is expected as the weather station is not yet recording data.

If you have a Tessel 2, you can follow a nice walkthrough to a web server project here: *http://tessel.github.io/t2-start/webserver.html*. The Tessel 2 web server also supports websockets, which will be discussed later in this chapter.

Server Live Reloading

When developing a server, it can be nice to automatically reload the server process. This should happen when the file *server.js* changes.

In Node.js, a good tool to achieve this goal is `nodemon`.

Let's install this next:

```
$ npm install nodemon
```

When you now run the server with:

```
$ nodemon server.js
```

You should see updates whenever you change the file *server.js* with an editor:

```
18 Aug 20:04:59 - [nodemon] v1.4.1
18 Aug 20:04:59 - [nodemon] to restart at any time, enter `rs`
18 Aug 20:04:59 - [nodemon] watching: *.*
18 Aug 20:04:59 - [nodemon] starting `node server.js`
18 Aug 20:07:17 - [nodemon] restarting due to changes...
18 Aug 20:07:17 - [nodemon] starting `node server.js`
```

Once we have a basic server, let's look how to wrap an embedded device.

Adding a Database

To store data from a sensor in the weather station, you need a database. A simple database for embedded devices is SQLite. SQLite is a file-based relational database management system (RDBMS). You can install and run SQLite with embedded Linux.

To connect to the database from JavaScript, you need a connection manager. In Node.js, a good choice is Knex. You can install it as follows:

```
$ npm install -g knex
$ npm install --save knex
$ npm install --save sqlite3
```

With the next step, you init a config file for the database connection:

```
$ knex init
Created ./knexfile.js
```

The config file can be adapted to your needs. In this case, let's only use the development version:

```
// knexfile.js
// update with your config settings.

module.exports = {

  development: {
    client: 'sqlite3',
    connection: {
      filename: './dev.sqlite3'
    }
  }
};
```

After the database connection is established, Knex provides tools to easily manage tables in a database. For the simple weather station, the plan is to use a database schema with two tables.

One table tracks measurements from a device and another table stores data snapshots from the sensors. In the language of SQL, this means a *measurement* has many *snapshots* and a *snapshot* belongs to a measurement.

To build this schema, Knex can help with simple scripts:

```
$ knex migrate:make createMeasurements
```

Then, you add the table data:

```
// migrations/createMeasurements
var table = function(t) {
    t.increments().primary();
    t.string('name');
    t.string('comment');
    t.timestamps();
}

exports.up = function(knex, Promise) {
  return knex.schema.createTable('measurements', table)
            .then(function () {
                console.log('Measurements table is created!');
            });
};

exports.down = function(knex, Promise) {
  return knex.schema
            .dropTable('measurements', table)
            .then(function () {
                console.log('Measurements table was dropped!');
            });
};
```

The *snapshots* table can be created with:

```
$ knex migrate:make createSnapshots
```

Then you need to define a schema for the snapshots as follows:

```
var table = function(table) {
    table.increments().primary();
    table.integer('time');
    table.integer('temp');
    table.integer('measurement_id')
        .references('id')
        .inTable('measurements');
    table.timestamps();
}

exports.up = function(knex, Promise) {
  return knex.schema
            .createTable('weather_events', table)
            .then(function () {
                console.log('weather events table is created!');
```

```
                });
        };

exports.down = function(knex, Promise) {
    return knex.schema
                .dropTable('weather_events', table)
                .then(function () {
                    console.log('weather events table was dropped!');
                });
};
```

To use this connection from other scripts, you need to add "models" with the Book-shelf.js ORM. For a simple weather station, two models will do: one for measurements and one for weather snapshots. Here is the measurements snapshot:

```
// models/measurement.js

// load the database config
var bookshelf = require('../config');
var Snapshot = require('./snapshot');

var Measurement = bookshelf.Model.extend({
    tableName: 'measurements',
    hasTimestamps: true,

    snapshots: function() {
        return this.hasMany('Snapshot');
    }
});
module.exports = bookshelf.model('Measurement', Measurement);
```

Next, the weather snapshot:

```
// models/snapshot.js

// load the database config
var bookshelf = require('../config');
var Measurement = require('./measurement');

var Snapshot = bookshelf.Model.extend({
    tableName: 'snapshots',
    hasTimestamps: true,

    measurements: function() {
        return this.hasMany('Measurement');
    }
});
module.exports = bookshelf.model('Snapshot', Snapshot);
```

To test this setup, you can create scripts to add new measurements and snapshots to the database:

```
// scripts/add_measurement.js
var bookshelf = require('./config');
var Measurement = require('./models/measurement');

var measurement = Measurement.forge({name: 'Sensor 1'});
measurement.save().
  then(function() {
    return bookshelf.knex.destroy();
});
```

Then run:

```
$ node scripts/add_measurement.js
```

Now, you can see an entry in the database:

```
$ sqlite3 dev.sqlite3
SQLite version 3.8.10.2 2015-05-20 18:17:19
Enter ".help" for usage hints.
sqlite> select * from measurements;
1|Sensor 1||1461187585457|1461187585457
```

And a similar script to add snapshots:

```
// scripts/add_measurement.js
var bookshelf = require('../config');
var Snapshot = require('../models/snapshot');

var snapshot = Snapshot.forge({measurement_id: 1, temp: 23});
snapshot
  .save()
  .then(function() {
    return bookshelf.knex.destroy();
});
```

Last, you need to integrate the database with the web server. Connecting the parts in file *server.js* can look like this:

```
// server_with_db.js
var express = require('express');
var bodyParser = require('body-parser');

// connect with db
var bookshelf = require('./config');
var Measurement = require('./models/measurement');

var port = 4000;

var app = express();
app.use(bodyParser.urlencoded({ extended: false }));
```

```
// basic routes
app.get('/', function(req, res) {
  res.writeHead(200);
  res.write('server is running');
  res.end();
});

// measurements
app.get('/measurements/:measurement_id', function(req, res) {
  res.writeHead(200);
  Measurement.collection().fetch({
    withRelated: ['snapshots']
  })
  .then(function(collection) {
      return collection.mapThen(function(model) {
        return model.toJSON();
      })
  })
  .then(function(results) {
    res.write(JSON.stringify(results, null, '  '));
    res.end();
  })
  .catch(function(e) {
    console.log(e);
    res.write('problem');
    res.end();
  });
});

app.post('/measurements', function(req, res) {
    var snapshot = Snapshot.forge({measurement_id: req.body.id,
                                   temp: req.body.temp});
    snapshot.save().
      then(function() {
        res.writeHead(200);
        res.write('snapshot saved');
        res.end();
      })
      .catch(function(err) {
        res.writeHead(200);
        res.write('problem saving snapshot');
        res.write(err);
        res.end();
      });
});

app.post('/measurements/:id', function(req, res) {
    var snapshot = Snapshot.forge({measurement_id: req.body.id,
                                   temp: req.body.temp});
    snapshot.save().
      then(function() {
        res.writeHead(200);
```

```
        res.write('snapshot saved');
        res.end();
    })
    .catch(function(err) {
      res.writeHead(200);
      res.write('problem saving snapshot');
      res.write(err);
      res.end();
    });
  });
});

var server = app.listen(port);
```

Now, the whole setup can be tested with the user agents from the weather display. To test this, you run:

```
// get measurements
$ node get_measurements.js
GET url: http://localhost:4000/measurements/1
[
 {
  "id": 1,
  "name": "Sensor 1",
  "created_at": 1461188045864,
  "updated_at": 1461188045864,
  "snapshots": [
   {
    "id": 1,
    "temp": 23,
    "measurement_id": 1,
    "created_at": 1461188049036,
    "updated_at": 1461188049036
   }
  ]
 }
}
```

Now you can post weather data from different places in a network. Let's take a look at how to post data from embedded devices to the measurement station.

The Transmission Control Protocol and User Datagram Protocol

While HTTP is very popular, there are more efficient network protocols for transporting data from sensors, including the *Transmission Control Protocol* (TCP) or the *User Datagram Protocol* (UDP).

TCP and UDP are very similar. The main difference is that TCP provides feedback on whether a packet was received, whereas UDP is "fire-and-forget," meaning a server does not know whether a client received the data. UDP can be a good choice when you want to stream data from sensors where you know that data redundancy is high enough. For example, if you are simply sending temperature readings from a room to a monitoring station, the "cheap" data transmissions from UPD might be acceptable.

Assuming an Intel Galileo connected via Ethernet, you can easily send UDP packages with the following server:

```
var five = require('johnny-five');
var Galileo = require('galileo-io');
var board = new five.Board({
  repl: false,
  io: new Galileo
});

var dgram = require('dgram');
var server = dgram.createSocket('udp4');

var port=9888;

var server, temperature;
board.on("ready", function() {

  startupServer();
  temperature = 0;

  // measure temperature with Grove sensor
  var temperature = new five.Thermometer({
    controller: 'GROVE',
    pin: "A1"
  });

  temperature.on("data", function() {
    if (temperature === Math.round(this.celsius)) {
      return;
    }
    var message = '' + temperature;
    temperature = Math.round(this.celsius);
  })
})

// send temperature
function sendTemperature(server, remote) {
  var message = new Buffer('Time: '
        + (new Date())
        + '  Temp: '
        + temperature + '\n');

  server.send(message, 0, message.length, remote.port, remote.address,
            function(err, bytes) {
    if (err) {
      console.log(err);
    } else {
      console.log('tx: ' + message);
```

```
    }
  });
}

function startupServer() {
  // handle main events from server
  server.on('listening', function () {
    var address = server.address();
    console.log('UDP Server listening on ' + address.address + ":" + address.port);
  });

  server.on('close', function () {
    console.log('Client closed connection');
  });

  server.on('message', function(message, remote) {
    for (var i=0; i<10; i++) {
      sendTemperature(server, remote);
    }
  });

  // bind server to port
  server.bind(port);
}
```

And on the client, you can have:

```
// subscribe_udp.js
var dgram = require('dgram');
var client = dgram.createSocket('udp4');
var address = 'galileo';
var port = 1288;

client.on('message', function (message, remote) {
  console.log(remote.address + ':' + remote.port +' - ' + message);
  client.close();
});

var message = new Buffer('request temp');
client.send(message, 0, message.length, port, address, function(err, bytes) {
  if (err) throw err;
  console.log('UDP message sent to ' + address +':'+ port);
});
```

If you now start the processes on both sides, you get:

```
$ node subscribe_udp.js
UDP message sent to galileo:1288
192.168.3.102:1288 - Time: Mon Jan 04 2016 20:40:25 GMT+0000 (UTC)  Temp: 21
```

Using Node.js modules, you can explore protocols and messages on a high level. Once your system works, it is possible to optimize other parameters such as system cost or size.

The WebSocket Protocol

Another important protocol for data transport is the WebSocket Protocol (RFC6455) (*https://tools.ietf.org/html/rfc6455*). In contrast to TCP and UDP, websockets is an application-level protocol that solves some problems with HTTP. Websockets are extensively used for building real-time web applications and have two advantages over using HTTP:

- Websockets add less communication overhead to a network because they do not use headers for every communication request.

- With websockets, you can listen for certain messages and push state directly to a client.

The examples using HTTP do not "automatically" update the state of an device. As a result, a user must fetch state "manually." For many situations, we want to broadcast data from an embedded device. This is when pushing state with websockets becomes interesting.

A number of Node modules for websockets exist. One interesting library is socket.io, which offers a number of fallbacks when websockets are not available. Websockets is one possible transport for socket.io (others are flashsocket, html file, xhr-polling, and jsonp-polling).

The WebSocket protocol negotiates over HTTP if an existing HTTP connection can be upgraded to bi-directional communication via a handshake. After a successfull handshake, client and server can send and receives messages at will.

The ws Module

To start, we are going to use the ws module. Install the module with:

```
$ npm install --save ws
```

Websockets provide bidirectional communication, which means you can send and receive messages with websockets. This is nice to control device outputs or to receive data from inputs such as sensors.

You can explore the workings of websockets for embedded devices with an Arduino and LED attached. To push data from that device with websockets, write the following:

```
var five = require('johnny-five');

var http = require('http');
var port = 4000;
```

```
var board = new five.Board({
  repl: false
});

// set up WebSocketServer to push bytes
function setupServer(board) {

// import a websocket server
var WebSocketServer = require('ws').Server;

// prepare server
var server = http.createServer(function (req, res) {
  res.write('ok');
  res.end();
}).listen(port);

var wss = new WebSocketServer({server: server});

// connection is set up
wss.on('connection', function(ws) {
    console.log('websocket connected');

  // incoming messages
      ws.on('message', function(message) {
        console.log('received: %s', message);
        var state = parseInt(message);
        state == 1 ? board.led.on() : board.led.off();
      });
  });
}

// start up connection
board.on('ready', function() {
  this.led = new five.Led(3);
  setupServer(this);
});
```

To test websockets from the command line, you can install a nice command-line tool called wscat:

```
$ npm install -g wscat
```

And run:

```
$ wscat -c ws://localhost:4000
connected (press CTRL+C to quit)
  > 1
  > 0
```

This should result in switching the LED on the embedded device. Similarly, you can "push" bytes from an embedded device to a websockets client. To see how this works, connect a button to the Arduino on pin 4.

Then you can add a button to the board object as follows:

```
board.on('ready', function() {
  this.button = new five.Button(9);
  setupServer(this);
});
```

And, hook into the button press event:

```
// set up WebSocketServer to push bytes
function setupServer(board) {

var WebSocketServer = require('ws').Server;

// prepare server
var server = http.createServer(function (req, res) {
  res.write('ok');
  res.end();
}).listen(port);

var wss = new WebSocketServer({server: server});

wss.on('connection', function connection(ws) {
    console.log('websocket connected');

    board.button.on('press', function() {
      ws.send('button push');
    });
  });
}
```

To see how it works, you simply make a connection to the web server. Now you can observe events from the button:

```
$ wscat -c ws://localhost:4000
connected (press CTRL+C to quit)
  < button push
  < button push
  < button push
```

Instead of the command-line tool wscat, you can write a small client with the ws module as follows:

```
var WebSocket = require('ws');

var client = new WebSocket('ws://localhost:4000');

client.on('open', function() {
  client.on('message', function() {
    console.log('push');
  });
});
```

Websockets are also handy to communicate between an embedded device and a web browser. Connections to the web browser will be explored in the next chapter.

Remote Procedure Calls over Websockets

Based on the WebSocket protocol, you build a medium for *remote procedure calls* (RPCs). With RPCs, you can invoke methods on objects that come from other devices. Figure 9-6 illustrates how this can be useful.

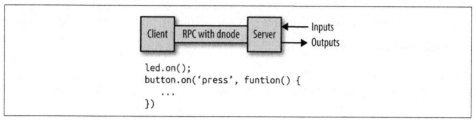

Figure 9-6. With RPCs, you can invoke functions from remote servers attached to outputs (LEDs, displays) and inputs (sensors)

To begin, take a simple board setup with an LED attached. Without RPCs involved, you can only control the objects within the scope of a script. The initial setup might look like this:

```
// led_control.js
var port = 4000;

// set up board
var five = require('johnny-five');

// select a board adapter
// var Edison = require('edison-io');
// var Galileo = require('galileo-io');
// var BeagleBone = require('beaglebone-io');

var board = new five.Board({
  // add the adapter here
  // io: new Galileo()
});

board.on("ready", function() {
  var led = new five.Led(3);

  this.repl.inject({
    led: led
  });
});
```

You can use the LED object on the device with the following commands:

```
# node led_control.js
1452444373827 Device(s) Intel Galileo Gen 2
1452444373883 Connected Intel Galileo Gen 2
1452444373969 Repl Initialized
>> led.on();
```

Now, with RPCs you can call the LED object from a different location and context in a network. To see how this works, you must build a web server with support for RPC.

One option is to use the dnode module by James Halliday. You can install this with:

```
$ npm install --save dnode
```

Then, wire up the server as follows:

```
// dnode_server.js
// port to listen to
var port = 4000;

// set up board
var five = require('johnny-five');

// board adapters
// var Edison = require('edison-io');
// var Galileo = require('galileo-io');
// var BeagleBone = require('beaglebone-io');

var board = new five.Board({
  repl: false
});

board.on("ready", function() {

    // place the pin connected to an LED
    this.led = new five.Led(13);

      // now start up server
      startupServer(this);
    });

function startupServer(board) {
  var dnode = require('dnode');
  var net = require('net');

    // create local web server
    var server = net.createServer(function(conn) {

    // set up RPC objects
    var rpc = dnode({

        // these functions can be invoked from other places
        ledOn: function() {
```

```
          console.log('on');
          board.led.on();
        },
        ledOff: function() {
          board.led.off();
        }
      });

      // connect local dnode objects with remote
      conn.pipe(rpc).pipe(conn);
      });

        server.listen(port, function() {
          console.log('Server running on port: ' + port);
        });
      }
```

And the client:

```
// dnode_client.js
var net = require('net');
var dnode = require('dnode');
var port = 4000;

var rpc = dnode();
rpc.on('remote', function (remote) {
  remote.ledOn(); // this function will be invoked on the server
});

var conn = net.connect(port, 'galileo');
conn.pipe(objects).pipe(conn);
```

Now you can turn the LED on and off from other places if you run:

```
$ node dnode_client.js
```

## CHAPTER 10

Web Frontends for Things

Screens and displays are useful ways to give a device user direction and feedback. Some embedded devices operate "headless," meaning without an attached display, which reduces the complexity and power requirements. Others build displays into the device design. Internet-connected and embedded devices can compromise: the device itself can be headless, but it can provide a display (and sometimes interactivity) on another Internet-connected device, such as a phone or computer. In this chapter, we'll discuss building displays and interactions with embedded devices through web browsers.

Web browsers render documents in HTML. Combined with JavaScript, HTML increasingly allows humans to interact with hardware remotely over a physical link or a network.

With the newer HTML5 standard, browsers also support new ways of rendering graphics and video. When HTML was first conceived in 1989, computers were dealing mainly with textual documents. The modern landscape has evolved to meet the ever-expanding variety of digital media. This chapter discusses some new concepts and special libraries to handle graphics with JavaScript.

For many programmers, the first steps into browser and graphical programming start with jQuery, a popular library that we will briefly review in this chapter. From there, separation between application state and rendering logic is discussed. This is commonly called the model-view-controller (MVC) pattern, and you will find some variations in the JavaScript community.

The Processing library for JavaScript P5.js offers the opportunity for new abstractions within browser experiences. As an example, you'll learn how graphics in a browser can be controlled by physical devices.

Adding Static Pages

In our discussion of network protocols in the previous chapter, most examples used the command line. While command-line user agents are great for development, users of devices generally prefer working with a web browser.

Web browsers render HTML documents that might contain information from embedded devices. Besides providing an output, web browsers can also capture user *input* with forms. In sum, serving HTML is an important task of web application development.

So far in this book, we have explored HTTP mainly to transport data to and from another machine. But HTTP can also transport "resources" that are interesting to users, such as text, pictures, or HTML. With HTML, you can provide forms, buttons, and other inputs to control the state of a device.

The easiest way to render an HTML page is as a "static page": a page whose content is not generated through a script but rendered just as it is stored.

Let's add ecstatic (*https://github.com/jfhbrook/node-ecstatic*), a Node.js middleware that can filter requests for static content. In a fresh directory, initialize Node with:

```
$ npm init -y
```

Then install `ecstatic` with:

```
$ npm install --save ecstatic
```

Next, in a file called *static/index.html*, save the following HTML:

```
<html>
  <head>
    <title>testpage</title>
  </head>
  <body>
    <form action="/api/message" method="POST">
      <textarea name="message"></textarea>
      <button type="submit">Update</button>
    </form>
  </body>
</html>
```

Based on the web server from Chapter 8, let's add a route to serve all files from the *static* directory:

```
// static_server.js
var ecstatic = require('ecstatic');
router.use(ecstatic({ root: __dirname + '/static' }));
```

Now you can serve a page of static HTML! Before you point your browser to the route localhost:3000, you should add a route to handle the form submission:

```
var message = '';
function updateMessage(err, body) {
  message = body.message;
}

var api = Router();
api.post('/message', function(req, res) {
  formBody(req, {}, updateMessage)
  res.writeHead(301, {Location: '/'});
  res.end();
});
router.use('/api', api);
```

To process the form, you must include a Node.js library to process data in the body of a form. In this example, the body module is used.

To see how everything works, you can now run the server:

```
$ node static_server.js
```

You should see something similar to Figure 10-1.

Figure 10-1. Update form

If you press the "update" button, the new message is sent back to the server. Once updated, the browser is redirected back to the form. With this web interface you can easily send commands to an embedded device. Static pages can be extended with JavaScript and jQuery to build interactive user interfaces. Let's discuss some basics next.

Basic jQuery

Browsers are nice because they render HTML documents that can be styled and include graphics. However, with different browser vendors, there are different APIs used to support rendering and browser events.

To improve compatibility of JavaScript APIs across web browsers, John Resig started work on jQuery in 2005. jQuery makes it easier to work with JavaScript in the browser on a number of fronts: with jQuery, you can easily select "nodes" in a rendered HTML document. Then, jQuery simplifies working with events from these nodes. Finally, jQuery provides shims for graphical effects in older browsers too.

Let's look at an example of a basic user interface that utilizes jQuery. When working on a frontend, the first thing you need is some basic HTML, from which you load JavaScript and stylesheets.

The basic user interface is provided by a static page. Here's a basic *index.html* file to get started:

```
<html>
  <head>
    <meta charset="utf-8">
    <meta http-equiv="X-UA-Compatible" content="IE=edge">
    <title>Blinking LED UI</title>

<style>
  body{
     font:500 14px/21px 'Helvetica Neue', Helvetica, Arials;
     padding:40px;
  }
</style>

  </head>
  <body>
  </body>
</html>
```

As a first example, let's create a web page button that can be used to toggle a light:

```
<p>Toggle the light</p>
<button id="toggle">Toggle!</button>
```

Next, let's add jQuery to the HTML:

```
<script src="https://cdnjs.cloudflare.com/ajax/libs/jquery/2.0.3/jquery.js">
</script>
```

In a web browser, JavaScript is imported with <script> tags. You can either serve JavaScript directly from your server, or if libraries are common enough, you will find a version on a *content delivery network* (CDN). With a CDN, you can use an online version of a JavaScript library instead of a local download. This can save time but requires a stable internet connection.

Now, we need to attach an event handler that is executed when a user clicks:

```
$('#toggle').click(function() {
    toggleLight();
});
```

Another way to deal with events is with the on(event, callback) idiom from earlier examples:

```
$('#toggle').on('click', function(e) {
    toggleLight();
})
```

The "on" syntax is common in JavaScript. You attach an "event handler" to an event. In this case, you observe "click" events from the button. When the event is fired, you will see an output in the developer console.

This toggleLight function can then make an Ajax request to the server:

```
var state=0;
function toggleLight() {
    state = !state;
    $.post('/LED', '{"led": ' + state + '}');
}
```

If you now go to the web browser and type *localhost:4000* into the address bar, you'll see a web page similar to the one shown in Figure 10-2.

If everything works, you'll now be able to switch LED 13 on and off.

Figure 10-2. Toggle the button to turn the light on/off

When events like the click event happen, you want to update other places on a page. To prevent cumbersome code, we'll next look at the model-view-controller (MVC) pattern. With the MVC pattern, you can easily "structure" events.

Adding the Model-View-Controller

The MVC is important only if you need to build more complicated user interfaces. You might want to skip this section and revisit it later if you prefer more artistic and experimental graphical setups at first.

In the previous example, the `toggleLight` function could grow quickly with user-facing features—for example, to make the click event update parts of the browser interface. For example, you might add code to the function to make the interface show if the LED is ON or OFF.

The MVC pattern was created to better structure user interfaces. In a nutshell, MVC is about separating abstract objects (i.e., "models") and the way they are rendered (i.e., "views"). "Controllers" provide a bridge for communication between views and models.

MVC is used to build all kinds of software interfaces, from large painting programs on workstations up to calendars on mobile phones. Over the last few years, MVC has also captured many aspects of web applications and user interactions in web browsers.

Although there are a number of JavaScript libraries that solve the MVC problem in browsers, one of the simplest ones to use is Backbone.js by Jeremy Ashkenas. Similar to Arduino, there is a large ecosystem around Backbone.js that facilitates building large projects, too.

Here is an overview of view and model classes in Backbone:

Backbone.View

A *view* renders things on a screen with a `render()` function. Additionally, the view captures events from a user, such as mouse clicks or key presses. `Back bone.View` is usually bound to a model. If the model changes, the view re-renders.

Backbone.Model

An abstract data model that captures state changes of objects. For example, if an LED should toggle from ON to OFF, a `Backbone.Model` sends notifications to its observers (a `Backbone.View`, for example).

Now, to make the previous page interactive, you need to load the Backbone.js libraries and its dependencies jQuery and Underscore.js first. You add these dependencies in the *static/index.html* file. We will add the links to the CDNs for these dependencies just below our jQuery CDN link:

```
<script src="https://cdnjs.cloudflare.com/ajax/libs/jquery/2.0.3/jquery.js">
</script>
<script
 src="https://cdnjs.cloudflare.com/ajax/libs/underscore.js/1.5.2/underscore-min.js">
</script>
<script
 src="https://cdnjs.cloudflare.com/ajax/libs/backbone.js/1.1.0/backbone-min.js">
</script>
```

While jQuery provides helpers to simplify the manipulation of a web page in the browser, Underscore.js fixes some weakenesses in the JavaScript language—for example, for iterating on collections or managing function scope.

 This tutorial doesn't go into a lot of detail on the libraries we're using, but we encourage you to check out the documentation and tutorials for those libraries in order to understand them better. The "Third-Party JavaScript" section of JavaScript for Cats (*http://jsfor cats.com/#third-party-javascript*) (a beginner introduction to JavaScript) offers a good introduction to the idea of plugins, and to Underscore.js in particular.

To show how this works, let's consider the following example. We'll create a "brighter" button that lets users brighten up the light, and a "darker" button that will dim the LED. Additionally, we'll render information about the state of the LED.

For this, you need two `Backbone.Views`—one view for the controls and one view for the status information:

```
var ControlsView = Backbone.View.extend({
  template: _.template('\
    <button id="darken">darken</button>  \
    <button id="brighten">brighten</button>  \
  '),
  events: {
    'click #brighten': 'handleBright',
    'click #darken': 'handleDarken'
  },
  handleBright: function() {
    this.model.brighten();
  },
  handleDarken: function() {
    this.model.darken();
  },
  render: function() {
    this.$el.html(this.template());
    return this;
  }
```

```
});

var StatusView = Backbone.View.extend({
  template: _.template('\
  <h1>Current intensity: <%= intensity %> \
  '),
  render: function() {
    this.$el.html(this.template({intensity: this.model.get('intensity')}));
  },
  initialize: function() {
    this.listenTo(this.model, 'change', this.render);
  }
});
```

Both views observe changes in the same model. While the `ControlsView` provides
buttons for changes, the `StatusView` should rerender after changes. The communication between the views happens through a model.

A simple model for the LED could look as follows:

```
var LEDModel = Backbone.Model.extend({
    defaults: {
    intensity: 0
  },
  url: '/LED',
  brighten: function() {
    var intensity = this.get('intensity');
    if (intensity < 255) {
      intensity++
    }
    this.set('intensity', intensity);
    this.save();
  },
  darken: function() {
    var intensity = this.get('intensity');
    if (intensity > 1) {
      intensity--
    }
    this.set('intensity', intensity);
    this.save();
  }
});
```

Last, you must tie everything together as follows (the views should listen to events
from the model):

```
var led = new LEDModel();
var controls = new ControlsView({el: '#controls', model: led});
var statusView = new StatusView({el: '#status', model: led});
```

And render everything:

```
$(document).ready(function() {
  controls.render();
  statusView.render();
});
```

When you now go to the browser, you should see something similar to the page shown in Figure 10-3.

Figure 10-3. Adjust light brightness with controls

You now have separation of concerns in terms of user-visible entities and communication to the server.

 More ideas about building web applications with Backbone.js can be found in the book *Full Stack Web Applications with Backbone.js* (O'Reilly, 2014). To get an idea of how the previous example might look for a small LED matrix, check out *http://vcard.pipefish book.com*. The editor can be used to translate visual pixels into hex numbers for a microcontroller.

Now let's look into another library for graphics and interactions in the browser.

Websockets in a Browser

Toggling state with HTTP is important, but more often, you want to subscribe to a device with real-time updates. For these cases, there are websockets.

A Bare Minimum Websocket Connection

For the following experiments, you need a server that sends updates from websockets. Based on the server examples from the previous chapter, this looks as follows:

```
// websockets_server.js
var express = require('express');
var morgan = require('morgan')('dev');
var ecstatic = require('ecstatic');

// set up server
var app = express();
app.use(morgan);
app.use(ecstatic({ root: __dirname + '/static' }));
var port = 4000;

// set up board
var five = require('johnny-five');

// adapters
// var Edison = require('edison-io');
// var Galileo = require('galileo-io');
// var BeagleBone = require('beaglebone-io');

var board = new five.Board({
    repl: false
});

board.on("ready", function() {
  var led = new five.Led(13);
  var slider = new five.Sensor("A1");
  led.blink(500);
  startupServer(slider);
});

function startupServer(slider) {
  // prepare server
  var server = app.listen(port);

    // sockets to push bytes
    var WebSocketServer = require('ws').Server;

    var wss = new WebSocketServer({server: server});

    wss.on('connection', function connection(ws) {
        console.log('websocket connected');
        ws.on('message', function incoming(message) {
          console.log('received: %s', message);
        });

        slider.scale([0, 100]).on("slide", function() {
```

```
        ws.send(JSON.stringify({data: this.value}));
      });
  });

    wss.on('close', function close() {
      console.log('disconnected');
    });
  }
```

Modern web browsers support the Websockets protocol very well. To subscribe to updates from a device, you use the following approach:

```html
<html>
  <head>
  <meta charset="utf-8">
  <meta http-equiv="X-UA-Compatible" content="IE=edge">
  <title>Blinking LED UI</title>

  <style>
   body{
      font:500 14px/21px 'Helvetica Neue', Helvetica, Arials;
      padding:40px;
   }
  </style>
<script src="https://cdnjs.cloudflare.com/ajax/libs/jquery/2.0.3/jquery.js">
</script>

</head>
<body>
 <div id="state"></div>

  <script>
   var ws = new WebSocket('ws://localhost:4000');
   ws.onmessage = function(e) {
     $('#state').html(e.data);
   };
  </script>
</html>
```

To show how this works, let's connect a potentiometer to a device:

Now, run the server with:

```
$ node server.js
```

When you go to the browser, you'll see updates from the device (see Figure 10-4).

Figure 10-4. Receive data from browser

The D3.js Library for Plotting Data

D3 is a popular JavaScript library written by Michael Bostock to visualize data in a web browser. D3 stands for "Data-Driven Documents." According to the D3 documentation, the library "allows you to bind arbitrary data to a Document Object Model (DOM), and then apply data-driven transformations to the document."

This means that D3 provides a means for mapping JavaScript arrays and objects to DOM elements that a web browser can render. To show how this works, let's consider a simple example of loading D3 and plotting data from a device.

First, you must set up an empty *index.html* and load D3. The easiest way to load D3 is by loading the script from a CDN, such as:

```
<script src="https://cdnjs.cloudflare.com/ajax/libs/d3/3.4.1/d3.min.js"></script>
```

Alternatively, you can copy the library from the GitHub repository (*http://github.com/mbostock/d3*) or the project website (*http://d3js.org*).

By adding a script reference to the library, you obtain a d3 object in the browser to work with.

The d3 object is somewhat similar to the $ object in jQuery. This means that you can select DOM nodes. And you can build new nodes with a .append. For drawing, you need an svg-based canvas first. Adding this "svg" is the first step to building a graph. Therefore, we define the following construct:

```
var vis = d3.select("#graph")
        .append("svg");
```

You can modify the canvas with attributes such as width and height of the graph with:

```
var w = 900,
    h = 400;
vis.attr("width", w)
   .attr("height", h);
```

We can also add text with:

```
vis.text("Our Graph")
   .select("#graph")
```

Next, let's plot some data. In D3, you start with data that might look like:

```
var dataset = [{coord: [10, 20, 30, 40]}];
```

The main point is that coordinates are wrapped in some property of a data element. The power of D3 is the "mapping" or "binding" of data to a visual language of shapes and colors. Besides data binding, the toolbox of D3 provides many abstractions and tricks to process data and set up basic user interactions.

Another important part of D3 is "chaining" commands. So, once you have bound data to properties of HTML or svg tags, you can add more visual transformations, or add event bindings.

Drawing a line with D3 might then look like:

```
<script>
  var dataset = [[0, 20, 0, 300], [0, 20, 0, 300]];

    var w = 900,
        h = 400;

    var vis;
    function setup() {
       vis = d3.select("#plot")
                  .append("svg");

       vis.attr("width", w)
          .attr("height", h);

       vis.text("The Plot")
           .select("#plot")
    }

    function draw(dataset) {
       vis.selectAll('line')
         .data(dataset)
         .enter()
         .append('line')
         .attr('stroke', '#000')
         .attr('x1', function(d) { return d[0] })
         .attr('y1', function(d) { return d[1] })
         .attr('x2', function(d) { return d[2] })
         .attr('y2', function(d) { return d[3] })
    }
    setup();
    draw(dataset);

    var ws = new WebSocket('ws://localhost:4000');
```

```
ws.onmessage = function(e) {
  var point = JSON.parse(e.data);
  dataset[1] = [point.data, 20, point.data, 300];
  vis.remove();
  setup();
  draw(dataset);
};

</script>
```

Notice how using D3 can easily abstract away the coordinate system. Generally, this simplifies focus and play with data instead of graphical layout of chart.

If everything works, you should see two lines, as shown in Figure 10-5. The coordinates of the second line can be controlled with a physical device, such as a slider on the Arduino.

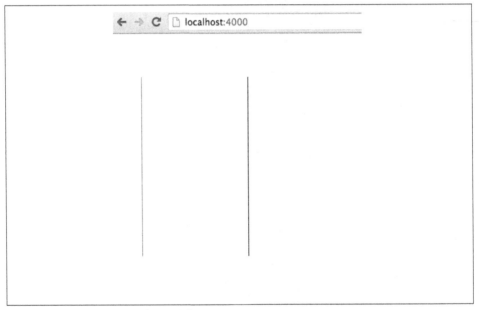

Figure 10-5. Drawing two lines with D3

D3 is also an important building block in projects dealing with data management, such as charting libraries as Epoch (*https://github.com/epochjs/epoch*).

P5.js

A very popular library for graphics is Processing, which has its roots in the Processing framework developed by Ben Fry and Casey Reas. As such, it has the same roots as the original Arduino IDE. There is also a Processing-inspired JavaScript library: P5.js (*https://github.com/processing/p5.js*).

P5.js gives you the possibility to create and mix media in a web browser with physical devices.

To get started, you need to add p5.js in a file called *static/index.html*:

```
<script src="http://cdnjs.cloudflare.com/ajax/libs/p5.js/0.4.19/p5.js"></script>
```

Then, you need to define a Processing "sketch." This looks similar to the Arduino IDE, as Processing and the Arduino IDE have the same roots.

To start, insert the following sketch:

```
<script>
  function setup() {
  }

  function draw() {
  }
</script>
```

The draw() function is repeated continuously, while the setup() function is only executed once. For example, you could draw a rotating rectangle with:

```
<script>
  var yPos = 0;

    function setup() {
      createCanvas(900, 600);
      x = width / 2;
      y = height;
      frameRate(30);
    }

    function draw() {
      background(20);
      rect(width/4, yPos, width/2, height/2);
    }

  // Connection with websockets
  var ws = new WebSocket('ws://localhost:4000');
  ws.onmessage = function(e) {
    var point = JSON.parse(e.data);
    yPos = point.data;
    console.log(yPos);
  };
</script>
```

This works very similar to the previous example with D3.js. The Arduino sends data from its analog input via sockets to the client. The client subscribes to the events from the websocket and updates the data points. The result is shown in Figure 10-6.

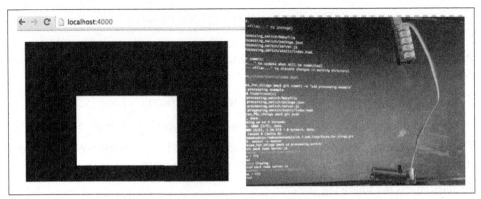

Figure 10-6. Controlling effects in the browser with Arduino and P5.js

Processing is great for all kinds of creative experiments. You could change the speed of the rectangle, let the rectangle rotate, or change the color. You might even want to play with video controls and the <video> tag in the browser.

## CHAPTER 11

Entering the Cloud

Now that we've examined some examples that worked on a local network, it is time to see how to connect devices across networks. Instead of sending messages between devices, a place in the network will act as a message broker. With a message broker, location of devices is just another abstraction.

The use case of message brokers is usually this: imagine a number of sensors in different houses or different cities. If these sensors used the *same* physical network, it would be difficult to collect data (this becomes less of a problem with new kinds of LoRaWAN networks). Instead, you need messages to travel via gateways or "message brokers" that are accessible from different locations.

To enable messaging across networks, a popular technology is the Message Queue Telemetry Transport (MQTT) protocol. With MQTT, you can apply the publish–subscribe pattern to multiple devices and locations. There are different ways to use MQTT. You can either set up an MQTT server, or you can rent services for message transmission.

The publish–subscribe software pattern provides the foundations for MQTT. It is not too difficult to implement publish–subscribe patterns with JavaScript yourself. With this, you'll see some more options to distribute state over a network, or to subscribe to updates from devices.

Publish–Subscribe Pattern

The publish–subscribe pattern is an important software design pattern for distributed systems. In a nutshell, it works similarly to a newspaper or an RSS feed. Many systems might be interested in news from different origins. As such, the newspaper acts as a publisher of messages that readers can then subscribe to. Figure 11-1 illustrates how this works.

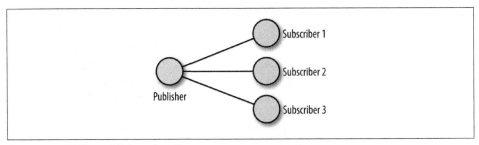

Figure 11-1. The publish–subscribe pattern

To show how useful this is, let's extend the dnode example from Chapter 9. Instead of a single link between one server and one client, you can now have multiple inputs and outputs to the Internet.

Let's start by reading a simple slider:

```
// simple_readout.js

// main publish function
function publish (ev, n) {
  console.log(ev + ': ' + n);
}

// set up board
var five = require('johnny-five');

var board = new five.Board({
  repl: false
});

board.on('ready', function() {
  var slider = new five.Sensor('A0');
  slider.scale([0, 200]).on('slide', function() {
    publish('slider', this.value);
  });
});
```

In this example, bytes are published from a slider. This is just a basic check that everything works:

```
$ node simple_readout.js
slider: 12.1231
slider: 130.13
```

To make the publisher notify subscribers, you can use EventEmitters from JavaScript, as follows:

```
// pub.js
var Hash = require('hashish');
var subscribers = {};
```

```
// the publishers calls the subscribers
function publish() {
  var args = arguments;
  Hash(subscribers).forEach(function(emit) {
    emit.apply(emit, args);
  });
}
```

To test this code, you can add subscriber callback functions:

```
// subscribers for testing purposes
subscribers.pete = function(ev, n) { console.log('pete.' + ev + ': ' + n) };
subscribers.carla = function(ev, n) { console.log('carla.' + ev + ': ' + n) };
```

To see how this works, you can run:

```
$ node pub.js
pm:pubsub pmu$ node pub
1452626939884 Device(s) /dev/cu.usbserial-AL01TQ7A
1452626939892 Connected /dev/cu.usbserial-AL01TQ7A
pete.slider: 79.17888563049853
carla.slider: 79.17888563049853
pete.button: 1452626945698
carla.button: 1452626946270
```

As a next step, you can broadcast data from the device via websockets to multiple clients. The following approach is based on dnode:

```
// pub_server.js
//
// simple pub-sub example inspired by
//    http://substack.net/roll_your_own_pubsub_with_dnode
//

// simple modules to iterate over subscribers
var Hash = require('hashish');
var subscribers = {};

// the publisher notifies the subscribers
function publish() {
  var args = arguments;
  Hash(subscribers).forEach(function(emit) {

    // call emit function from subscriber
    emit.apply(emit, args);
  });
}

// board is publisher
//     button on digital input: D4
//     slider on analog input: A0
//
var five = require('johnny-five');
```

```
var board = new five.Board({
  repl: false
});

board.on('ready', function() {

  var slider = new five.Sensor('A0');
  var button = new five.Button(4);

  slider.scale([0, 200]).on('slide', function() {
    publish('slider', this.value);
  });

  button.on('press', function() {
    publish('button', new Date().getTime());
  });
});


// start up dnode server
var dnode = require('dnode');

dnode(function(client, conn) {

  // generate callback function for subscribers

  // subscribers pass an emit function
  this.subscribe = function(emit) {
    console.log('new connection:  ' + conn.id);

    // publishers wants call emit function
    subscribers[conn.id] = emit;

    // cleanup if connection closes
    conn.on('end', function () {
      delete subscribers[conn.id];
    });
  };
}).listen(5050);
```

The publisher on the server calls the `emit` function from subscribers. You can use dnode to enter the context of the server with a `remote` object. With this, you can add subscribers from multiple processes. To show how this works, you can write a simple command-line client as follows:

```
// client.js
//
// sample dnode client
//    inspired by http://substack.net/roll_your_own_pubsub_with_dnode

var dnode = require('dnode');
var EventEmitter = require('events').EventEmitter;
```

```javascript
// enter server context with remote object
dnode.connect(5050, function(remote) {

  // prepare subscriber to capture events from server
  var subscriber = new EventEmitter;

  // capture slider event
  subscriber.on('slider', function(n) {
    console.log('slider: ' + n);
  });

  // capture button event
  subscriber.on('button', function(n) {
    console.log('button: ' + n);
  });

  // all other events
  subscriber.on('all', function(ev) {
    console.log(ev);
  });

  // attach this context to the emitter
  var emitter = subscriber.emit.bind(subscriber);

  // add subscriber to remote publisher
  remote.subscribe(emitter);

  // from client to server
  // remote.write('test');
});
```

Now, you could easily modify the client to specifically subscribe to events from only a button or a slider. The main obstacle with this publish–subscribe approach right now is that the subscriber must still be *within the same network*.

To overcome this, you need to learn about extending the publish–subscribe pattern with a *message broker*.

The MQTT Protocol

In contrast to the detailed headers of the HTTP, the MQTT protocol uses only a two-byte header. MQ stands for "messaging queue" and TT for "telemetry transport." It is much more common to use the abbreviation MQTT.

Early development of MQTT was done by Andy Stanford-Clark and Arlen Nipper at IBM in 1999. Their research was about transporting data from remote measurement sites, usually places that are hard for humans to access, such as oil fields.

Although MQTT was originally highly specialized, it is now quite popular for connecting all kinds of devices. In a sense, MQTT enables the publish–subscribe pattern across networks. This is different from previous examples, where data and its monitoring happened within the same network.

Figure 11-2 provides a visual representation of how this works.

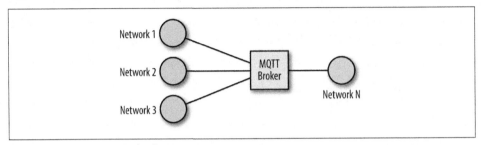

Figure 11-2. An MQTT broker

A simple example of MQTT might be a device to monitor temperature, light, and humidity (e.g., in a greenhouse), while capturing data at another node in the network.

The nodes that send data are "publishers," while nodes that capture data are called "subscribers." Data publishers and subscribers must have access to the same message broker.

Connecting to an MQTT Broker

An easy way to see MQTT in action is from the command line with the Node.js library MQTT.js, connecting to an MQTT broker.

There are several brokers available for free testing. A popular one is test.moquitto.org.

A message broker can also run on an embedded device, such as a Raspberry Pi or Intel Galileo. Some boards with embedded Linux have MQTT preinstalled.

To explore MQTT, let's install the MQTT.js library with:

```
$ npm install -g mqtt
```

When you can connect to a public broker for testing, you can see all kinds of messages. Let's subscribe to messages from a popular MQTT broker for testing: test.mosquitto.org.

Messages on a broker are grouped into "topics." Topics can have multiple levels like device/sensors/temperature:

```
$ mqtt subscribe -v -h test.mosquitto.org '#'
ajiang/demo MQTT 通信机制
command_from_grm dimmer
command_from_grm/1 left
edison/config {"enabled":"true"}
foo/bar hallo
```

To query a broker for messages, you can use wildcards for topics. For example, when you apply a #, it will match all topics from a root element:

```
$ mqtt subscribe -v -h test.mosquitto.org 'location/#'
location/me/b26a9d441622a657 {"_type": "location", "lat": "30.4884162",
"lon": "-97.6870723", "tst": "1450271909", "acc": "33.0"}
location/mm {"cog":-1,"batt":"45","lon":"-0.0819448","acc":"431",
"vel":-1,"vac":33,"lat":"51.5144","t":"u","tst":"1433351164","alt":18,
"_type":"location","tid":"mc"}
```

If you use +, you can filter for topics as follows:

```
$ mqtt subscribe -v -h test.mosquitto.org 'location/+/b26a9d441622a657'
location/me/b26a9d441622a657 {"_type": "location", "lat": "30.4884162",
"lon": "-97.6870723", "tst": "1450271909", "acc": "33.0"}
```

Instead of looking at messages from others, let's get going with our own simple messaging example. There are MQTT libraries for most boards with network access.

To *publish* messages with MQTT, you can also use the following command:

```
$ mqtt publish -v -h test.mosquitto.org 'location/pm' 'munich'
```

Playing with these commands is good preparation for the material to come.

Publish Messages

Instead of using MQTT.js from the command line, you can require the library as a dependency in a script:

```
var mqtt = require('mqtt');
var client = mqtt.connect('mqtt://test.mosca.io');

client.on('connect', function() {
  client.publish('location/device1', 'munich');
  client.end();
});
```

Let's extend this basic example by having a device publish messages.

First, let's build a data *publisher*:

```
// pub_arduino.js
//
var mqtt = require('mqtt');
var client = mqtt.connect('mqtt://test.mosquitto.org', 1883);
var five = require('johnny-five');

    // add board
    var board = new five.Board({
    repl: false
    });

board.on('ready', function() {
    client.publish('arduino', 'connected');

    // connect a sensor to an analog input
    var sensor = five.Sensor({
      pin: 'A5'
    });

    // Publish a message
    sensor.on('data', function() {
      var message = 'value: ' + this.value;
      client.publish('arduino/slider', message);
    });
});
```

This code now publishes a message to the Arduino topic on the MQTT channel. You can capture that data from another device—for example, to light an LED.

Subscribe to Updates

On a laptop, you could capture data from publishers. Let's *subscribe* to the data channel:

```
// mqtt_sub_10s.js
//
var mqtt = require('mqtt');

// create an MQTT client
client = mqtt.connect('mqtt://test.mosquitto.org', 1883);

// indicate what topics we care about
client.subscribe('arduino/#');

// respond to message on subscribed topic(s)
client.on('message', function (topic, message) {
  console.log(topic,": ", message.toString());
});

// exit after 10s whether or not we get a message
```

```
setTimeout(function() {
  client.end();
}, 10000);
```

If everything works, you see:

```
$ node mqtt_sub_10s.js
arduino/slider :  value: 312
arduino/slider :  value: 412
arduino/slider :  value: 553
```

MQTT Server with Mosca

Instead of using public MQTT brokers, you can write your own MQTT server with Node.js. One such option is Mosca (*https://www.npmjs.com/package/mosca*).

To use Mosca, you must install a persistence store such as Ascoltatori (*https://www.npmjs.com/package/ascoltatori*). Using this package, Mosca supports several options, including MongoDB and Redis.

Redis is easy to install and even runs on most embedded devices. You could also use VPS, or an EC2 server at Amazon, for example, and send updates from devices everywhere in the world.

Mosca can run standalone or "embedded" inside a Node.js application.

To run Mosca inside a Node.js application use this:

```
var mosca = require('mosca')

var ascoltatore = {
  type: 'redis',
  redis: require('redis'),
  db: 12,
  port: 6379,
  return_buffers: true, // to handle binary payloads
  host: "localhost"
};

var moscaSettings = {
  port: 1883,
  backend: ascoltatore,
  persistence: {
    factory: mosca.persistence.Redis
  }
};

var server = new mosca.Server(moscaSettings);
server.on('ready', setup);

server.on('clientConnected', function(client) {
    console.log('client connected', client.id);
```

```
    });

    // fired when a message is received
    server.on('published', function(packet, client) {
      console.log('Published', packet.payload);
    });

    // fired when the mqtt server is ready
    function setup() {
      console.log('Mosca server is up and running')
    }
```

Now you can start the server with:

```
vagrant@vagrant-ubuntu-trusty-64:~/.nvm$ mosca -v
      +++.+++:    ,+++    +++;   '+++    +++.
    ++.+++.++   ++.++  ++,'+  `+',++  ++,++
   +`  +,  +: .+  .+ +;  +; '+ '+ +`  +`
   +`  +.  +: ,+  `+ ++  +; '+ ;+ +   +.
   +`  +.  +: ,+  `+ +'    '+      +   +.
   +`  +.  +: ,+  `+ :+.   '+    +++++.
   +`  +.  +: ,+  `+  ++   '+    +++++.
   +`  +.  +: ,+  `+   ++  '+    +   +.
   +`  +.  +: ,+  `+ +:  +: '+ ;+ +   +.
   +`  +.  +: .+  .+ +;  +; '+ '+ +   +.
   +`  +.  +: ++;++  ++'++   ++'+' +   +.
   +`  +.  +:  +++   +++.   ,++'   +   +.
{"name":"mosca","hostname":"vagrant","pid":7999,"level":30,"mqtt":1883,
      "msg":"server started","time":"2015-12-08T22:19:31.985Z","v":0}
{"name":"mosca","hostname":"vagrant","pid":7999,"client":"mqttjs_ef3","level":30,"
      msg":"client connected","time":"2015-12-08T22:19:32.287Z","v":0}
```

Having your own MQTT server allows you to tune the broker to your needs—for example, to process messages more quickly or more reliably. The MQTT protocol supports "levels of quality." Jan-Piet Mens's slidedeck for "MQTT for Sysadmins" (*https://speakerdeck.com/jpmens/mqtt-for-sysadmins*) offers a good introduction to the topic.

Cloud Services

Running your own servers in the cloud is not for everyone. It often requires time to install, secure, and maintain servers. Instead of running your own servers, you could rent services in the cloud.

CloudMQTT

If you want to try a hosted MQTT service, a good start is CloudMQTT (*http://cloudmqtt.com*). You must sign up (*https://customer.cloudmqtt.com/customer/signup?p=1*) for an account first, where you will get a username and password to use private channels.

Then, similar to the free testing service `test.mosquitto.org`, you can use the command line to test your channel.

First, to subscribe to the channel in one terminal:

```
$ mqtt sub -h m20.cloudmqtt.com -p 12001 \
            -P <password> -u <user> -t "/welcome/hello" -v
```

And, in another terminal, you can publish messages for testing:

```
$ mqtt pub -h m20.cloudmqtt.com -p 12001 \
            -P <password> -u <user> -t "/welcome/hello" -m "123"
```

Now, you should see your message in the first terminal window as follows:

```
hello
```

HiveMQ

HiveMQ is an MQTT broker that targets enterprise use cases. In addition to MQTT for the enterprise, HiveMQ offers a number of development tools.

There is a public broker `broker.hivemq.com` for development of MQTT services, and there is a browser-based MQTT client (*http://hivemq.com/demos/websocket-client*). Both can be handy when you develop a new service.

PubNub

PubNub is more than a pure MQTT broker. It allows you to send messages in real time over networks.

Entering PubNub with MQTT is a nice start. Pubnub provides an MQTT broker as discussed in the previous sections; however, compared to the previous brokers, Pub-Nub uses IDs for the channel names. You can see the special message format at Pub-Nub with:

```
$ mqtt sub -v -h mqtt.pubnub.com '#'
pub-c-11817d38-b172-45f3-8214-280d8af48492/
    sub-c-394a95fc-1cf5-11e5-a5e2-02ee2ddab7fe/my_channel 888PPM
pub-c-11817d38-b172-45f3-8214-280d8af48492/
    sub-c-394a95fc-1cf5-11e5-a5e2-02ee2ddab7fe/test 888PPM
```

PubNub uses a "publish key" and a "subscribe key" for the topic name. With this, it is hard for attackers to guess channel names. Instead of exploring MQTT with PubNub (*https://www.pubnub.com/blog/2014-07-08-mqtt-now-supported-by-pubnub*) further, let's now look at how to work with PubNub in real time.

To learn more about using PubNub, get its JavaScript library (*https://github.com/ pubnub/javascript*). The library gives us an object to send and receive messages. Here is an example from the Publish–Subscribe tutorial (*https://www.pubnub.com/develop ers/tutorials/publish-subscribe*):

```
// publish a simple message to the demo_tutorial channel
PUBNUB_demo.publish({
channel: 'demo_tutorial',
    message: {"color":"blue"}
});
```

Telegram

Telegram is a messaging platform similar to WhatsApp. However, Telegram offers a "bot API" that allows you to send and receive messags from an embedded device. With this, you can quickly control devices from your mobile phone.

To use Telegram, you must sign up for an account with an app on your mobile phone. The Telegram app is available for both Android and iOS.

Telegram offers good support for creating a message bot, as shown in Figure 11-3.

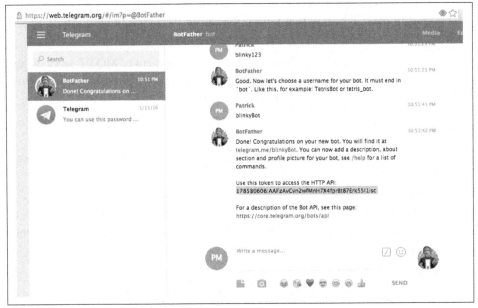

Figure 11-3. The "BotFather" helps you to obtain an API key

With this API key, you can use a couple of Node.js modules to interact with Telegram. These modules are nicely described by Rafael Specht da Silva (*https://medium.com/@rssilva/talking-with-arduino-using-telegram-and-javascript-d874a0b560cb#.ipjgp9oif*).

For example, to connect an LED to your bot, you can write:

```
// led-on.js
```

```
// use Johnny-Five for hardware
```

```
var five = require('johnny-five');

// create the Telegram bot
var TelegramBot = require('node-telegram-bot-api');
var johnnyTelegram = require('johnny-telegram');
var token = '<API_TOKEN_HERE>';

var bot = new TelegramBot(token, {polling: true});

var board = new five.Board();

// instantiates the module and passes the telegram bot as parameter
johnnyTelegram.init(bot);

// waits until the Johnny-Five board is ready. Creating sensors
// before it is ready will probably cause execution errors
board.on('ready', function () {

    // instantiate a new LED
    var led = new five.Led(3);

    // we are adding an LED to Johnny-Telegram called 'led' so we have a
    // reference name to call on Telegram
    johnnyTelegram.add('led', led);

    // this method adds a listener to the telegram events
    johnnyTelegram.bindEvents();
});
```

You can start the service with:

```
$ node led-on.js
```

This server will automatically connect to Telegram. And, from Telegram, you now can send messages to your device with:

```
call led on
call led off
call led blink
```

Instead of calling remote functions, you could also read out sensor data:

```
// read_sensor.js
var johnnyTelegram = require('johnny-telegram');

var five = require('johnny-five');
var TelegramBot = require('node-telegram-bot-api');
var board = new five.Board();
var token = '<API_TOKEN_HERE>';
var bot = new TelegramBot(token, {polling: true});
johnnyTelegram.init(bot);

board.on('ready', function () {
    // instantiate a sensor
```

```
var sensor = new five.Sensor({
  pin: 'A5'
});

// adds a sensor named 'sensor'
johnnyTelegram.add('sensor', sensor);

// every time that this sensor has data,
// call the Johnny-Telegram 'setValue' method
// setting the 'sensor' sensor stored value
proximity.on('data', function() {
  console.log(this.value);
  johnnyTelegram.setValue('sensor', this.value);
});

johnnyTelegram.bindEvents();
});
```

Now, to obtain this value from the sensor from your message, you can send a message to the Telegram bot:

```
value sensor
5
```

Temboo

Temboo allows easy integration of Arduino and other boards with cloud services such as Twitter and others. By using Temboo, you can easily wrap existing APIs. Working with Temboo, you can quickly get some working examples of reading and writing messages to Twitter, for example. To get started, go to the Temboo installation page (*https://temboo.com/arduino/others/library-installation*).

System Design with NodeRED

NodeRED advertises itself as "a visual tool for wiring the Internet of Things." The focus is on a "visual programming" approach where you can easily connect devices and services. NodeRED is one of the first open IoT design systems, and the framework is built with Node.js so that you can run it wherever you want.

The authors Nick O'Leary (*https://twitter.com/knolleary*) and Dave Conway-Jones (*https://twitter.com/ceejay*) developed NodeRED at IBM Emerging Technology and released it to GitHub in 2013. NodeRED projects can run standalone on SBCs or can be easily integrated into cloud services, such as the IBM Bluemix environment. Bluemix provides special Bluemix node types to make integration of devices easier. Besides Bluemix, there are cloud providers such as "fred" (free node red) (*https://fred.sensetecnic.com*) where you can immediately get a running instance at no cost.

NodeRED should work easily on your laptop or any kind of SBC with Linux. NodeRED runs well on small Linux systems such as BeagleBone and Raspberry Pi, and it is quite easy to set up a federated set of servers exchanging messages with each other.

Install NodeRED

You can easily install NodeRED with npm:

```
$ sudo npm install -g nodered
```

Then run:

```
$ node-red
```

Concepts

The visual interface of NodeRED is a web GUI served by default at port 1880. This makes it easy to design systems from a web browser.

As you can see in Figure 11-4, the GUI contains a list of NodeRED elements to the left, and on the right, there is a debug console and a "deploy" button to put the current system live.

Figure 11-4. The NodeRED GUI with different components on the left

To design a system, you drag components from the left side of the screen onto an active tab. Then, you link them together by dragging links between them. In the parlance of NodeRED, a program is called a FLOW and a step is called a NODE.

Each node can be either an INPUT node, an OUTPUT node, or a PROCESS node. Typically, an INPUT node starts a FLOW. It often takes its input from an external source and always has at least one output. In the example shown in Figure 11-5 the input is a Twitter search for the term "javascript."

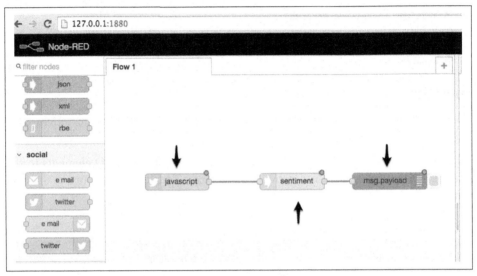

Figure 11-5. Different node types: input, process, and output

A PROCESS node has one input and at least one output. It always takes its input from another node. In this example, the input is the output from the Twitter feed and the node is performing sentiment analysis on it.

An OUTPUT node typically ends a flow. It takes its input from another node and passes its output to an external target. In this example, the output is going to the "debug console." You can pipe debug output to the server process too.

The data that is passed from node to node is called a MESSAGE. A message is a JSON object with at least one element called "payload." There can be more root elements though. In this example, the message contains the element "topic."

An example of the actual data sent from a Twitter feed called "antwerp" looks like this:

```
1 Mar 13:36:35 - [info] [debug:2f55a60b.8dc4aa]
{ score: 2,
  comparative: 0.11764705882352941,
  tokens:
   [ 'we',
     'are',
     'proud',
     'to',
     'announce',
     'the',
     'opening',
     'of',
     'two',
     'new',
     'showrooms'
   ],
  words: [ 'proud' ],
  positive: [ 'proud' ],
  negative: [] }
21 Mar 13:36:35 - [info] [debug:e0ea087c.1e9748]
We are proud to announce the opening of two new showrooms in Munich and Antwerp
https://t.co/J2ORDi4l6U https://t.co/WGRcb0o4b0
```

One of the nice things about NodeRED is that the flows are stored in JSON format in a plain-text file. That means that sharing flows with colleagues is a simple matter of copying your flow or part of a flow and sending it to your coworker, where they can paste it in.

All nodes and flows are in a standard folder format, so it is simple to extend the system with your own flows based on any available Node.js library.

 You can extend this example to blink an LED according to Twitter sentiments, as demonstrated in "Tweet Sentiment to LED Using Node-RED" on Hackster.io (*https://www.hackster.io/punch-through/ tweet-sentiment-to-led-using-node-red-6a380a*).

New node types can be found either by crawling GitHub for NodeRED nodes or by looking on sites such as *http://flows.nodered.org*.

If you want to add nodes yourself, you can to go to the *nodes* folder under your NodeRED installaton and find two sample files: an HTML file for the visual UI and a JavaScript file for the functionality.

## CHAPTER 12

Making Robots with Node.js

The NodeBots (*http://nodebots.io*) movement is all about creating robots using Java-Script and Node.js. The focus is typically on making something that works as quickly and easily as possible. From a learning perspective, this is inspiring and engaging—you have the ability to create something new in just a few hours! This can be extremely empowering, especially when you consider that hardware is often an intimidating field to enter. Because NodeBots use high-level languages, you can create a robot on your first day.

Robots exist in all forms and categories. Researchers in robotics, such as Rodney Brooks, professor emeritus for robotics at MIT, suggest that robotics will create new kinds of professions.[1] On the flipside, robots might provoke a number of discussions that will challenge the classical view of work and play.

For now, building robots with JavaScript leans more toward play and prototyping. But before going into practical examples, let's explore some concepts and motivations for Nodebots.

What Is a Robot?

When people think of robots, they think of a physical device performing "programmed actions." Programmed actions can include motion, sound, or blinking parts.

The motion of mechanical devices can evoke very human-like expressions, as demonstrated by the Sony dancing robots (*https://www.youtube.com/watch?v=9vwZ5FQEUFg*). In addition to novel actions like dancing, robots can also serve

---

[1] See Rodney Brooks, "Why we will rely on robots", TED conference, filmed Feb 2013 (*https://www.ted.com/talks/rodney_brooks_why_we_will_rely_on_robots?language=en*).

some "useful" function, such as feeding your cat when you are not at home or industrial uses such as building an automotive part.

From a computer science perspective, robots are based on several abstractions, as illustrated in Figure 12-1.

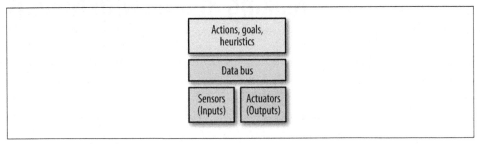

Figure 12-1. Robot abstractions

At the lowest levels, robots are made of actuators and sensors.

An *actuator* is a part that converts energy into motion. There are different types of actuators. For example, the motors that turn the wheels on a remote control car are rotational actuators. Your bicep muscle is a linear actuator.

A *sensor* is an input to the system in the form of data about the environment. For example, your phone knows which direction is down by reading which axis of its accelerometer most closely matches Earth's gravitational pull.

 Building robots requires a multidisciplinary approach. You need to have an understanding of the *mechanics* of motion. You may need motors (and gears possibly) before anything can move. To control motors, you'll need to explore *electronics*. Finally, you must be able to communicate with a robot through *software*.

From a hardware perspective, building a robot is about putting together a system of inputs (sensors) and outputs (actuators). These parts communicate over a data bus, such as I2C or SPI. Robots can perform actions depending on the inputs and their plans and heuristics (decision-making processes).

Why Build Robots in Node.js?

Depending on your background, there are different reasons Node.js is a good choice for creating robots.

Community

In Node.js, we are accustomed to plugging together pieces of code (other people's Node.js modules) to build our projects. This is normal practice in programming, and many programming languages flourish because their users share their libraries (e.g., for Ruby, there are Ruby Gems; for Python, there is Rust; etc.).

One of Node.js's biggest advantages is that npm makes it so convenient for the community to create and share code components they have created. You saw examples of hardware libraries in Chapter 8, but robots need special libraries for actuators and sensors. With Node.js, more often that not, you can find a library to reuse in your own project so that you can save time and get up and running quickly.

 Libraries such as Johnny-Five provide a nice starting point into the Nodebots community (not least because of good documentation and tutorials at *http://nodeschool.io*). Rick Waldron first presented ideas behind Johnny-Five at NodeConf 2012 (*https://www.youtube.com/watch?v=jf-cEB3U2UQ*). Raquel Velez has presented Vektor, a library for kinematics in JavaScript. Raquel discusses the general idea of JavaScript robotics in her talk at LXJS 2013 (*https://www.youtube.com/watch?v=SssnWZzLGvo*).

Education

One reason it is interesting to use Node.js for robotics is the educational context.

In traditional electronics and low-level programming languages, it might take you a full session to learn how to blink an LED. It's the "Hello, World!" of hardware, and extremely useful if you need to debug a circuit. However, if all you learned on your first day of programming was how to print "Hello, World!", you would probably not be inspired to try something more complex.

JavaScript robotics are high level enough that you should be able to go beyond one blinking light to building a robot on your first day.

Building a robot on your first day shows you that you are capable of creating something interesting and possibly unique. It's a starting point. It makes you think about how you could take it further, do it better. "Sure I made a robot car," you think. "Now can I control it from the Internet? Can I let Twitch.tv drive it? Would it respond better if I took a look at the module I'm using to run the servos? What if it had some obstacle-avoiding intelligence onboard?" Because you already have a base project, these new capabilities are approachable as small, fun, new features.

Product Development

From a design and entrepreneurship standpoint, you want to get to a minimum viable product, or proof of concept, as quickly as possible. Building *quickly* means plugging prebuilt pieces together, getting prompt feedback, and using modularity to swap in different ideas and interactions.

A Nodebot can help you answer questions like: Is the thing that I have made interesting? What could it be worth to someone? Would it be better if I changed this or that aspect of the design?

By using a dynamic language such as JavaScript, you can prove the merits of your idea—and if you're so inclined, show potential investors or teammates what you mean when you describe your vision.

As with robots for education, building a NodeBot for product development is a beginning, not necessarily an end result. JavaScript and pluggable components help you understand the scope and value of the thing you are trying to accomplish. And then you can build up, tear down, or iterate from there.

The Tessel Project

To build robots, you need hardware. If you are new to hardware, the activation energy might be too high to get started.

You might be able to buy a sensor or a component, but it can feel like starting from scratch every time: get the component, read the datasheet, and figure out what its power requirements are and how to turn it on.

Arduino libraries challenge this notion, but the Arduino programming language is still relatively low level. Moreover, there is no single system for the community to contribute libraries or organize a project with, such as a manifest file like the *package.json* from a project in Node.js.

However, Node.js libraries for hardware components is an increasing phenomenon. The open source Tessel Project (*https://tessel.io*) in particular creates modular components (such as a climate sensor) that easily plug into microcontroller boards and come with npm installable libraries. The project also explicitly promotes community-created modules: npm libraries for commodity hardware parts, such as breakout boards from Adafruit and SparkFun, along with community-member instructions on how to wire the component. You can see Tessel modules and community modules at *http://tessel.io/modules*. Tessel modules let you quickly experiment with motors, sensors, and other components without having to think too much about underlying mechanics or electronics (see Figure 12-2).

Figure 12-2. Tessel 2 with servo module and a community-contributed motion sensor

When you want to start building a robot with Tessel, take a look at the following modules:

Servo module (https://tessel.io/modules#module-servo)
   The servo module is based on a PCA9685 (*https://www.adafruit.com/datasheets/ PCA9685.pdf*) PWM controller. This module also provides a power plug to drive motors from an external power supply. Managing power is important when working with motors, as forces and voltages from a motor can potentially harm a micrcontroller.

Relay module (https://tessel.io/modules#module-relay)
   The relay module can help you to power on/off devices from a standard 220V power plug. This means you can take existing electronic devices like a floor lamp, a toaster, or an industrial machine and make them part of your robot's output. The relay connects these things to your JavaScript code.

Distance sensors
   For driving robots, it is often important to detect obstacles. The community-contributed modules SEN10737p (*https://tessel.io/modules#tessel-sen10737p*) and HCSR04 (*https://tessel.io/modules#proximity-hcsr04*) are nice plug-and-play distance-sensing solutions.

Potentiometer

To simulate values from sensors, potentiometers can often be helpful. Currently there are no Tessel modules with potentiometers and ADC, but you can easily build one yourself.

These are helpful for a traditional robot that might move and react to the environment. But you can also push the boundaries: what about a robot that moves in response to something else? Maybe it reacts to sound or warmth, like animals do. What if it reacts to information from the Internet, like a Twitter feed? Or what about a simple data-collecting robot that provides input to a system's online code, like a motion detector that emails you when something moves? Internet access provides powerful input and output tools to any robotic system.

Some examples of this are:

- Hot enough text (*https://www.hackster.io/ifoundthemeaningoflife/hot-enough-text-93575e*) sends you a text through Twilio when the water on your stove is boiling
- Flinching robot (*https://www.hackster.io/ifoundthemeaningoflife/flinching-robot-b1bfa2*) runs away from loud noises
- RFID webapp authorization (*https://www.hackster.io/ifoundthemeaningoflife/rfid-authorization-9841b9*) provides security by only letting you view a site if an authorized card is present
- Website down alarm (*https://www.hackster.io/ifoundthemeaningoflife/website-down-alarm-4a9b8b*) brings the digital world into the physical space by turning on an alarm if your website doesn't return a 200 OK response when it is pinged

If you'd like to get involved in the Nodebots community, check out this map of Nodebots meetup groups (*http://nodebots.meetup.com*).

Robot Kits

In addition to a microcontroller and electronics to control actuators, you will often need some motors to get started with robots. In "Actuators" on page 101, you saw different motors you can use. In the language of electronics, motors are "actuators," as they convert energy into motion.

Hackster.io lets authors define "robot kits" on each of their projects. For example, if you scroll down to the "Things Used in This Project" (*https://www.hackster.io/ifoundthemeaningoflife/ website-down-alarm-4a9b8b*) section of the Website Down Alarm project, you'll see that it has purchase links for every component! You could buy the parts, use the code from GitHub, and follow the instructions to make your own alarm very easily. The combination of shareable or commodity hardware components with open source software libraries and instruction kits shares the vision of 3D printing: "make your own, at home." If you have a 3D printer, you can make any of thousands of open source inanimate objects. If you have software libraries, purchasable components, and possibly a 3D printer, you can make and collaborate on thousands of smart, useful objects.

Motors and Potentiometers

In principle, you can begin working with robots by putting together a simple "kit"— all you need to do is connect a servo motor to a microcontroller. If you want to detect distance to objects or provide motion feedback, you can do so by simply adding a potentiometer to this setup.

Robots often need multiple motors, and the Tessel Servo Module from Figure 12-2 is a great way to get the power and PWM signals you need for up to 16 servos. Even though the module is designed for Tessel, many people also throw the module into systems using Raspberry Pi or Arduino because it's easier than building a servo controller from scratch.

Servo motors are typically controlled with PWM. We'll look at some examples of motor control with JavaScript momentarily.

Sumobot Jr.

There are a number of projects for robotic vehicles available today. One popular open source option is Pawel Szymczykowski's Sumobot Jr. (*https://github.com/makenai/ sumobot-jr*) (see Figure 12-3).

The Sumobot Jr. provides a great laser-cuttable design that you can adapt to do just about whatever you want.

Although you might not have a laser cutter of your own, most maker spacers offer courses on how to laser cut parts. Another place to get your parts is Ponoko (*https:// www.ponoko.com*), or you can even buy a small laser cutter for home usage such as Mr. Beam (*http://mr-beam.org*). If you're interested in learning more, check out Pawel's Sumobot Jr. assembly video (*https://www.youtube.com/watch? v=0Q3hrKUwxDM*).

Figure 12-3. An assembled Sumobot Jr.

Hackarobot

The Hackarobot design was funded via a Kickstarter campaign in 2014 (*https://www.kickstarter.com/projects/hackarobot/hackabot-nano-compact-plug-and-play-arduino-robot*). This robot is based on an Arduino Nano together with DC motors, sensors for proximity (HC-SR04), and an MPU6050 with an accelerometer.

You can buy the Hackarobot (Figure 12-4) from its creator Thomas Lee via Tindie (*https://www.tindie.com/products/HackARobot/hackabot-nano-arduino-compatible-robot-kit*).

Figure 12-4. The Hackarobot comes with sensors and a Bluetooth module

Example Project: The Robot Claw

As you can see in Figure 12-5, the simple robot claw built for this example consists of a mechanical frame combined with servo motors.

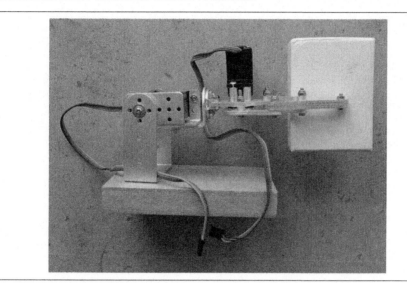

Figure 12-5. A simple robot claw with servo motors

The following provides direct control of servo motors:

```
// direct_arm.js
var five = require("johnny-five");

var board = new five.Board({
});

board.on("ready", function() {

    // arm servo on pin 9
    var arm = new five.Servo(9);

    // hand servo on pin 10
    var hand = new five.Servo(10);

    this.repl.inject({
      hand: hand,
      arm: arm
    });
});
```

You can then add "actions" to combine control of multiple servo motors:

```javascript
// add_actions.js
var five = require("johnny-five");
var util = require('util');

var board = new five.Board({
});

// create a new Arm class
var Arm = function() {

    five.Servo.apply(this, arguments);

    this.up = function() {
      this.max();
    }

    this.moveTo = function(pos) {
      this.to(pos);
    }

    this.down = function() {
      this.min();
    }
};
util.inherits(Arm, five.Servo);

// create a new Hand class
var Hand = function() {
  five.Servo.apply(this, arguments);

    this.open = function() {
      this.min();
    }

    this.moveTo = function(pos) {
      this.to(pos);
    }

    this.close = function() {
      this.max();
    }
};
util.inherits(Hand, five.Servo);

board.on("ready", function() {
  // arm servo on pin 9
  var arm = new Arm(9);

  // hand servo on pin 10
  var hand = new Hand(10);
```

```
    this.repl.inject({
      hand: hand,
      arm: arm
    });
  });
```

Let's try the movements in the Node.js read-eval-print loop:

```
$ node hello_action.js
1453555335508 Device(s) /dev/cu.usbmodem14131
 1453555335518 Connected /dev/cu.usbmodem14131

 1453555339060 Repl Initialized
>> hand.open()
>> hand.close()
>> arm.up()
>> hand.open()
```

To make more complex movements, you can combine multiple actions into "goals":

```
// add_goals.js
var five = require("johnny-five");
var util = require('util');

var board = new five.Board({
});

// create a new Arm class
var Arm = function() {

    five.Servo.apply(this, arguments);

    this.up = function() {
      this.max();
    }

    this.moveTo = function(pos) {
      this.to(pos);
    }

    this.down = function() {
      this.min();
    }
};
util.inherits(Arm, five.Servo);

// create a new Hand class
var Hand = function() {

    five.Servo.apply(this, arguments);

    this.open = function() {
      this.min();
    }
```

```
    this.moveTo = function(pos) {
      this.to(pos);
    }

    this.close = function() {
      this.max();
    }
};
util.inherits(Hand, five.Servo);

var Goal = function(arm, hand) {
  this.arm = arm;
  this.hand = hand;

    this.prepare = function() {
      this.arm.down();
      this.hand.open();
      console.log('prepared');
    }

    this.grabObject = function() {
      console.log('hand will close');
      this.hand.close();
    }

    this.moveObject = function() {
      this.arm.up();
    }

    this.releaseObject = function() {
      this.hand.open();
    }
}

// connect to Arm object
board.on("ready", function() {

    // arm servo on pin 9
    var arm = new Arm(9);

    // hand servo on pin 10
    var hand = new Hand(10);

    // add goal
    var goal = new Goal(arm, hand);

    this.repl.inject({
      hand: hand,
      arm: arm,
      goal: goal
```

```
        });
    });
```

Try it out:

```
>> goal.prepare()
>> goal.grabObject()
>> goal.moveObject()
>> goal.releaseObject()
>> goal.grabObject()
>> goal.prepare()
```

This robot claw provides provides two axes of freedom. With three axes of freedom, kinematics starts getting interesting—it provides a way to calculate movements on the basis of predefined coordinates. If you'd like to learn more about complex robotics, check out the tharp package (*https://www.npmjs.com/package/tharp*).

Example Project: Move a Vehicle

In addition to actuators, it's important to enable your robot to capture sensor data.

There is a Node/Tessel library to control a robot of a vehicle built around two continuous servo motors: servo-car (*https://www.npmjs.com/package/servo-car*) for general use and RC-Sumobot (*https://github.com/Frijol/RC-Sumobot*) for controlling it over a websocket.

Servo

```
var tessel = require('tessel');
var servolib = require('servo-pca9685');

var servo = servolib.use(tessel.port['D']);

var servo1 = 1;

servo.on('ready', function() {

    var position = 0;
    var dir = 0.05;

    servo.configure(servo1, 0.05, 0.11, function() {

        setInterval(function() {

            servo.move(servo1, position);

            if (position > 1 || position < 0) {
                dir = -dir;
            }
            position += dir;
```

```
        }, 100);

    });

});
```

MD25 Motor Shield

For real-world usage, you need larger DC motors to drive a vehicle. The Veter robot (*http://veterobot.com*) is a nice example of a moving vehicle. The robot controls different motors via I2C signals. You can build your own robot as shown in Figure 12-6 with the instructions at *http://veterobot.com/buildyourself.html*.

Figure 12-6. A robot using an MD25 motor shield and Intel Edison (based on the design of http://veterobot.com)

## CHAPTER 13

Wireless Data with Bluetooth

When you hear the term *Bluetooth*, you might think first of telephone headsets, speakers, computer mice, or keyboards. These have nothing to do with Internet connections, right? Right. At least at first glance. However, closer examination reveals that Bluetooth may have a role to play in Internet-connected devices.

One of the hurdles of data transmission with WiFi is the need to set up an Internet connection, often manually, by selecting a network or providing a network password. This often hinders the design and development of connected experiences. Bluetooth has the potential to ease entry into a connected system. With Bluetooth, you can connect directly to devices, skipping configuration of networks or Internet access points. You can then build clever gateways to provide small data packages, depending on your location or profile.

The Bluetooth Low Energy Protocol

There are two kinds of Bluetooth currently in common use: the high-bandwidth Bluetooth popularized for telephone headsets, and the newer Bluetooth Low Energy (BLE), also known as Smart Bluetooth and Bluetooth 4.0. The two protocols are entirely different from each other (*https://tessel.io/blog/94173952967/you-probably-dont-need-an-ibeacon*). Both can be used for building "smart" objects, but BLE is more common in IoT applications due to its low power consumption. Here are a few Bluetooth-based IoT applications:

- Bluetooth can be used for discovering and identifying devices and services such as data from physical objects. This data can help to make information from elsewhere apparent/visible/tangible in your physical surroundings—for example, a tempescope can visualize weather conditions, or BLE beacons can be strategically placed in a store to let customers know of current promotions.

- It can help to control things in the range of the Bluetooth radio, which is typically around 10–30 meters depending on how many other devices and humans communicate. This can be nice for automated lighting systems and robots that fly (small drones) or drive (small vehicles).

 Bluetooth is named after Harald Bluetooth, King of Denmark (*https://en.wikipedia.org/wiki/Harald_Bluetooth*). The king's name served as a placeholder for the project name when the technology was developped in the research labs of Ericsson in the 1990s. Bluetooth was first used to connect headphones to phones, but quickly spread into different realms of wireless data transmission.

The Bluetooth Low Energy protocol stack (*https://www.bluetooth.com/specifications/ bluetooth-core-specification*), shown in Figure 13-1, can be a bit daunting to understand at first. To adapt to the needs of IoT applications, additional specs (*https:// www.bluetooth.com/specifications/adopted-specifications*) have been introduced.

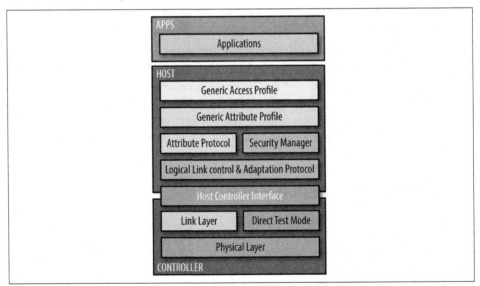

Figure 13-1. The Bluetooth Low Energy Protocol stack (source: https://www.blue tooth.com/specifications/bluetooth-core-specification)

From a software perspective, we are interested mainly in the upper layers of the Bluetooth protocol stack. But the underlying layers are important for application design as well, especially if you want to buy hardware for your products.

In Figure 13-1, you can see that the protocol stack builds on three main layers:

Application layer
Applications can use Bluetooth to communicate with remote devices (i.e., asking for or providing data). To help you understand this process, imagine a conversation between applications as strings of bytes. These strings of bytes can take two modes. Either they advertise properties to "scanning" devices, or they provide connections between devices.

Host layer
To assemble the string of bytes, there are abstractions such as "generic profiles" and "attributes." These abstractions provide information about the broadcasting device—whether it is a watch or light, for example.

Controller layer
On the lowest layer (*https://developer.bluetooth.org/TechnologyOverview/Pages/HCI.aspx*), data is transmitted without intimate knowledge of the data. This is done with circuits and chips that handle the Bluetooth radio signals.

The host and controller can be integrated on the same chip or can be separated. The bridge between host and controller is called the host-controller-interface (HCI) around which some tools are built (such as the hcitool).

To understand the different aspects of the host and application layers, it is necessary to look at the communication modes between devices. This will help you get a better feeling for the profiles and attributes of Bluetooth devices.

Communication Modes

When it comes to communication, devices act either as a *central* or a *peripheral*. A common "central" is your smartphone, which can scan for or control peripherals in your environment. Examples of "peripherals" are smart watches or some connected lightbulbs. The location of a device can be identified from the signal strength between devices.

With BLE, communication can happen in two modes. The first mode is the "advertisement" mode, as shown in Figure 13-2. In this mode, a peripheral advertises data packages that might be interesting to centrals. For this, no pairing (or connection) is necessary. While the peripheral advertises its services, the central can capture the packages through scanning their environment. This communication mode is what makes so-called Bluetooth "beacons" work.

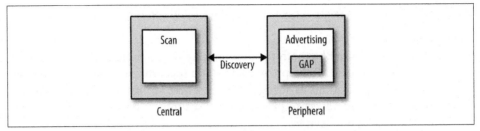

Figure 13-2. The advertisement mode

When a central and peripheral device *connect*, they enter the second BLE communication mode. In this mode, data can be transmitted through services and characteristics, as shown in Figure 13-3.

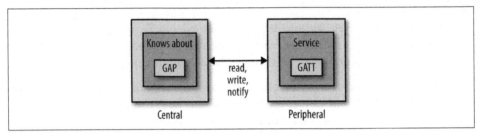

Figure 13-3. Connection mode

When devices are connected, *services* are the main grounds for communication. A service says something about the main features of a device and are identified by universally unique identifiers (UUIDs). To get a sense of services and some official UUIDs, take a look at the Bluetooth SIG list (*https://developer.bluetooth.org/gatt/serv ices/Pages/ServicesHome.aspx*). In addition to the official list of 16-bit-long UUIDs, you can define your own services with 128-bit UUIDs.

The generic attribute protocol (GATT) defines a generic hierarchy of data that a peripheral exposes. Attributes are identified with 128-bit unique IDs. These are called "characteristics," and they define whether data can be written or read, and how to notify a device about changes. A characteristic can have one or many attributes. Each attribute in a characteristic has a unique identifier.

GATT clients may use the attribute identifier to access and modify it. This is done with "write" and "read" operations.

Connect with Centrals

Many mobile phones come with Smart Bluetooth technology by default, which makes mobile phones a good starting point for exploring Bluetooth.

The smartphone typically plays the role of a central, which connects to a peripheral. Support of Bluetooth on smartphones depends on both the operating system and its underlying chipset. Many smartphones, particularly older Android devices, do not support BLE protocols out of the box.

When you work with a smartphone, apps play an important role. You will find a number of apps to discover BLE services in the Play store or on iTunes (LightBlue is a good example on iOS).

If you don't have a smartphone with BLE support, you can also use a Raspberry Pi, Intel Edison, or Tessel to act as central.

Installing Bluez

To work with Bluetooth on an SBC, you typically need to install a Bluetooth protocol stack including drivers. The most widely used project is the Bluez library.

The latest Bluez library can be downloaded from:

```
# wget https://www.kernel.org/pub/linux/bluetooth/bluez-5.24.tar.xz
```

Then you can build the library with:

```
# tar -xf bluez-5.24.tar.xz
# cd bluez-5.24
# ./configure --disable-systemd –disable-udev
# make
# make install
```

You can then run tools like `hciconfig` or `gattools` to interact with Bluetooth. On an Intel Edison, you must unblock Bluetooth drivers first with:

```
# rfkill unblock bluetooth
# hciconfig
hci0:   Type: BR/EDR  Bus: UART
BD Address: 98:4F:EE:03:38:9C  ACL MTU: 1021:8  SCO MTU: 64:1
UP RUNNING PSCAN
RX bytes:640 acl:0 sco:0 events:35 errors:0
TX bytes:975 acl:0 sco:0 commands:35 errors:0
```

Then you can launch to start scanning for devices around you:

```
# hcitool lescan
```

On Tessel 2, you don't need to do any special setup for BLE—just plug in a USB BLE dongle and use the `noble` Node module. See an example here: *http://tessel.github.io/ t2-start/modules/ble.html*.

Many smartphones can also act as peripherals. For example, when you control music from your smart watch on a smartphone, the phone is a peripheral to the watch. Modern smartphones also support a beacon mode to broadcast presence. In some cases, it is not possible to turn the device into a peripheral because of chipset limitations.

Another option to work with Bluetooth devices around you is via a web browser. With modern browsers, you can discover beacons through the new Web Bluetooth API. For example, Opera supports some operations to query profiles (*https:// dev.opera.com/articles/web-bluetooth-intro*). Also, Google Chrome allows you to connect to a device and query characteristics (*https://developers.google.com/web/updates/ 2015/07/interact-with-ble-devices-on-the-web?hl=en*).

Beacons

Beacons emit data, such as an ID or other attributes. In this way, they can tell other devices something about data in the environment. The format of the beacon's advertising data plays a special role and varies between different companies. The most famous beacon formats are Apple's iBeacon and Google's EddyStone, though there are also other specifications including the open source AltBeacon (*http://altbeacon.org*).

Invented by Apple, the iBeacon standard describes a special form of advertising of data from devices. Scanning devices pick these sequences of bytes up and can compare them against an external database. The data contains "major" and "minor" identifiers, which are used to differentiate individual stores and locations, respectively.

Invented by Google, the Eddystone specs describe advertisement of URLs. The specs can be found here: *https://github.com/google/eddystone/blob/master/protocol-specification.md*. Eddystone is one of the cornerstones of Google's Physical Web, an initiative to make physical objects "smart" by having each broadcast an associated URL.

To develop applications with beacons, you need some hardware, such as the options shown in Figure 13-4. There are also cheaper options that offer a nice start in Bluetooth-based experiences.

The Gimbal beacons (*https://store.gimbal.com*) by Qualcomm support both the iBeacon and Eddystone standards. The Gimbal beacons are interesting for their size, price, and battery life. For a nice tutorial on using Gimbal beacons with Node.js, check out "Beacon Tracking with Node.js and Raspberry Pi" (*https://medium.com/ truth-labs/beacon-tracking-with-node-js-and-raspberry-pi-794afa880318#*).

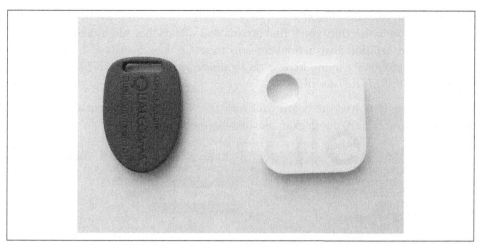

Figure 13-4. The Gimbal (left) and Tile (right) are just two examples of BLE beacons

RedBear Shields and Boards

If you are looking for Bluetooth hardware comparable to Arduino, RedBear Labs offers a nice collection of Bluetooth boards:

RedBear Duo

In this recent Kickstarter project, RedBear included a BLE module and a WiFi module, as shown in Figure 13-5. The board is similar to a Particle. As you can see in the figure, it is possible to add batteries on the VIN pins of the board as shown. This makes the boards suitable to design responsive environments.

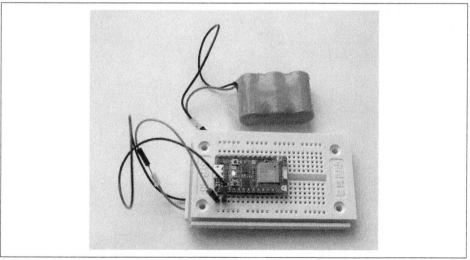

Figure 13-5. The RedBear Duo powered by a battery supports BLE, WiFi, and Arduino

RedBear Blend, Micro, and Mini

In addition to the Duo, you'll find boards and shields that add Bluetooth capabilities to an Arduino. Instructions for how to set up these boards with the Arduino Board manager are found here: *https://github.com/RedBearLab/Blend* and *https://github.com/RedBearLab/nRF8001*.

Once you have imported the board data with the Arduino board manager, you have access to a number of Arduino examples, as shown in Figure 13-6.

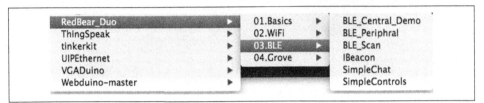

Figure 13-6. Arduino BLE examples from RedBear board

As many Arduino boards are based on a Nordic Semiconductor nRF_8001, there exists a special Node.js library to interact with these Bluetooth devices. It can be found at *https://github.com/sandeepmistry/arduino-BLEPeripheral*.

BlueIOT

The BlueIOT module is based on the BlueGiga BLE113, as shown in Figure 13-7.

Figure 13-7. BlueIOT board from fab-lab.eu (via tindie.com)

It has a couple of advantages compared to other solutions:

- BlueIOT has a very small form factor and can be powered from a coin cell battery, and sleeping currents can be smaller than 1 uA.
- It uses a FCC/Bluetooth-certified BLE module. This can save you time and costs if you want to develop your own BLE products later.
- The module comes with an ATmega328p chip that can be easily programmed with the Arduino toolchain.
- It is possible to update the module with OTA and connectivity configuration could be scripted with bgscript. This helps to separate application logic and communication logic, as well as reduce the load on the host processor.

Libraries for Bluetooth

Now that we've covered the hardware, it's time to discuss different strategies for developing software for Bluetooth solutions.

Arduino

Arduino provides a nice language to work with bits and bytes of Bluetooth as well as the microcontroller. Most of the identifiers can easily be coded in arrays of bytes. You can then attach Arduino functions to protocols from Arduino.

Let's look at a code example for building a Bluetooth beacon first with a RedBear Duo:

```
// redbear_beacon.ino
static advParams_t adv_params;

// When advertising, use these 128 bits
static uint8_t adv_data[31]={0x02,0x01,0x06, 0x1A,0xFF,0x4C,0x00,
0x02,0x15,0x71,0x3d,0x00,0x00,0x50,0x3e,0x4c,0x75,0xba,0x94,0x31,
0x48,0xf1,0x8d,0x94,0x1e,0x00,0x00,0x00,0x00,0xC5};

void setup()
{
    Serial.begin(115200);
    delay(5000);
    Serial.println("IBeacon demo.");
    ble.debugLogger(true);
    ble.init();

    adv_params.adv_int_min = 0x00A0;
    adv_params.adv_int_max = 0x01A0;
    adv_params.adv_type    = 3;
    adv_params.dir_addr_type = 0;
```

```
        memset(adv_params.dir_addr,0,6);
        adv_params.channel_map = 0x07;
        adv_params.filter_policy = 0x00;

        ble.setAdvParams(&adv_params);

        ble.setAdvData(sizeof(adv_data), adv_data);

        ble.startAdvertising();
        Serial.println("BLE start advertising.");
    }

    void loop()
    {

    }
```

You can discover this beacon with a BLE central. In Node.js, you can use a library such as a command-line utility (*https://www.npmjs.com/package/ibeacon-cli*) to start the scan process:

```
$ ibeacon
iBeacon command line utility

Options:
    -h, --help        Displays this message
    -v, --version     Displays the version
    -s, --scan        Scan for iBeacons
    -b, --broadcast   Broadcast as an iBeacon
    -u, --uuid        Proximity UUID
```

To scan a RedBear Duo Bean, you can use:

```
$ ibeacon -scan
Starting scan
bleacon found: {"uuid":"713d0000503e4c75ba943148f18d941e",
    "major":0,"minor":0,"measuredPower":-59,
    "rssi":-71,"accuracy":2.134232534620913,
    "proximity":"near"}
```

BLE Scanner and Parser

If you use a Raspberry Pi, Intel Edison, or Linux machine with the Bluez tool installed (see "Installing Bluez" on page 201), you can easily start scanning for BLE devices around you:

```
// ble_scan.js
var Scanner = require("ble-scanner");
var bleParser = require('ble-packet-parser');

var device = "scanner";
var callback = function(packet) {
    // packet is an array with hex values
```

```
      console.log( "Received Packet: " + packet);
      json = bleParser(packet);
      console.log(json);
   }

   // create new Scanner
   var bleScanner = new Scanner(device,callback);
```

You can then run this script:

```
# node ble_scan.js
```

And see something like:

```
HCICONFIG: succesfully brought up device scanner
HCIDUMP: cleared (code 0)
HCITOOL: cleared (code 0)
Received Packet: 04,3E,2B,02,01,03,01,A6,...
{ Event_Code: 62,
  Subevent_Code: 2,
  Packet_Length: 43,
  Reports:
   [ { eventType: 3,
       addressType: 1,
       address: '32:BF:50:C1:FB:A6',
       data: [Object],
       rssi: -77 } ] }
```

To make better sense of the low-level bytes of the BLE protocol, the Noble.js library
(discussed in the following section) is more helpful.

Noble.js

With Noble.js, you can easily explore Bluetooth services from any computer that runs
Node.js. The library comes with some helpful Getting Started documentation (*https://
github.com/sandeepmistry/noble/wiki/Getting-started*).

On an Edison, you must prepare the Bluetooth radio. The easiest way to make sure it
is running is to switch it on and off:

```
# rfkill unblock bluetooth
```

Tessel 2 also uses the Noble.js library for its BLE getting started experience (*http://
tessel.github.io/t2-start/modules/ble.html*).

Noble allows you to discover, read, and write characteristics from peripherals.

Let's first look at a simple scan for discovery of devices:

```
// simple_scan.js
var noble=require('noble');

// to keep track if the radio is powered or not
noble.on('stateChange', function(state) {
```

```
// radio must be powered on
    if (state === 'poweredOn') {
      noble.startScanning([], false);
    }
    else {
      console.log('stop scanning');
      noble.stopScanning();
    }
});

noble.on('discover', function(peripheral) {
    console.log('Found device with local name: ' +
        peripheral.advertisement.localName);
    console.log('advertising the following
        service uuid\'s: ' + peripheral.advertisement.serviceUuids);
});
```

Next, you want to see the details of a service. You can do this with:

```
$ node scan_services.js
poweredOn
found device: eddie2
   services: ec00
```

Bleno.js

In BLE, the "GATT server" serves the peripheral's attributes. The Bleno library lets you use a computer to act as a GATT in order to easily test BLE peripherals.

On GitHub, the library is described as "a Node.js module for implementing BLE peripherals." Similar to Noble.js, you must first start the radio and then wait for the connection:

```
// act_as_beacon.js
bleno.on('stateChange', function(state) {
    console.log('on -> stateChange: ' + state);

    // Start advertising
    if (state === 'poweredOn') {
        bleno.startAdvertising('Beacon', [customService.uuid]);
    }
});
```

Example Project: Proximity Detection

In this section, we'll use our new technical abilities (coupled with a library that helps you get information about the location of a device) to address a concrete human need: humans, physiologically, are bad at paying attention. Direct, concentrated focus is difficult to achieve in the face of even minor distraction, and compared to a computer we are not nearly as efficient at processing pure information. With this in mind, let's now take a look at robots that assess your environment and adapt to you.

 "Ubiquitous computing" and "calm technology" are terms coined by Mark Weiser (*http://www.ubiq.com/hypertext/weiser/ UbiHome.html*) to discuss what technology of the future might look like. This area of research explores the concept of humans as parts of a whole technological system. This concept is presented with some prototype applications in Kelsey Breseman's 2014 talk "Beyond the Screen: Humans as Input and Output" (*https:// www.youtube.com/watch?v=LdATa51ejgM*), where she urges technologists to "create technology you can forget about."

The Nest thermostat and the August lock are two fairly prescient examples of passive technology—that is, technology that magically works even without your input into the system.

For example, with an August lock installed, your front door can magically open for you in response to discovery of your smart watch or smartphone's BLE profile. Nest is meant to learn your habits and temperature preferences over time, and adapt itself into a system you can ignore.

In web programming, this type of responsiveness is familiar: an API call triggering an event in response to new information, or webhooks that republish a site based on a GitHub merge. How do we expand this type of system into physical space? It's intuitive: physical actions already occur in response to events. By making web-connected sensors and actuators, we bridge the gap between two systems that are already event-driven.

The August Lock approach could be extended to turn lights/audio/heaters/anything on and off based on the presence of the user's devices. For example, a database could have the device IDs for the smartphones of everyone in an office. The first employee to arrive at the office would trigger not just the lock but the power to the building's systems, and it could shut off again after the last employee leaves the office.

BLE Proximity-Based Switch

With little effort, you can build a relay switch when an authorized BLE device (or several!) is in range. You get to specify the BLE device(s) you want to activate the switch.

To get started with JavaScript, take a look at the following code from Kelsey Breseman's Hackster.io project BLE Proximity-Based Switch (*https://tessel.hackster.io/ ifoundthemeaningoflife/ble-proximity-switch-f5df21*):

```
// Based on examples from Kelsey Breseman:

var Ble = require('./ble_helpers.js');

var acceptedDevices = [
  "94:a1:a2:b3:ad:e3"
];

var ble = new Ble(acceptedDevices);
ble.scan();
```

The code wraps a BLE helper as shown here: *https://github.com/embeddednodejs/ ch_13_physical_internet/blob/master/proximity_check/ble_helpers.js*.

## CHAPTER 14

Toward the Physical Internet

In the previous chapter, our foray into building robots was mainly focused on connecting *inputs* (sensors for motion, proximity, etc.) and *outputs* (motors, displays, LEDs, etc.). In this chapter, we'll expand our work with single robotic devices to use robots as building blocks for shared experiences.

JavaScript was born in a web browser. What happens when web interfaces and robots merge? To give you some ideas, this chapter will introduce concepts and provide context to help address human needs with new technologies. This is important but hard to do. A famous example is the Apple Newton handheld device that was developed in 1993, long before smartphones became popular. The device was discontinued in 1998, but by adding a web browser, music, and more features, smartphones are estimated to populate the pockets of around two billion people today.

This chapter explores a few perspectives on the increasingly connected world we're building, and gives some example projects on how you can become an active participant in creating this connected society.

What Are Shared Experiences?

If you use Twitter or Facebook, you can see shared experiences as the connections you make when you "like" or "retweet" messages in your social network. Shared experiences allow humans to connect and form new kinds of communities. With the help of robots, shared experiences get physical.

For example, you could build a simple light setup that flashes when someone tweets at you. Or, with complex devices, you can track the flow of people, things, and information around you or across the Earth.

The idea of connecting humans through robotic devices has earlier origins than Facebook. The science behind feedback systems is called cybernetics, and it emerged in the 1940s with new kinds of radar technologies. Broadly speaking, cybernetic researchers study systems between man and machines. These systems may be distributed around the world. The idea that they work in concert often sounds like science fiction. Yet, if you look closely, a connected world is already in place:

- Every time you swipe a credit card, you authorize yourself with a connected network and your digital balance changes.

- Google may do analytics on search terms, but companies like Salesforce and NetSuite move the world by tracking people and objects across corporations.

- In your home, you might have a thermostat or lights you can control from your phone, or a lock that automatically unlocks itself as your Bluetooth-enabled device approaches.

- Tesla cars are noticeably Internet-connected in that you can download updates such as the relatively new self-driving highway features. In the future, driving experiences will increasingly be defined by monitors, counters, and gauges for sensors not only for physical quantities, but also for abstract entities like traffic or tourist attractions.

How do we move from digital experiences to physical (and vice versa)? The Internet has already demonstrated how near-instant massive exchanges of information can create systems and efficiencies previously undreamt of. By making devices that identify themselves online, update their own statuses, and even take action based on incoming information, we can create a world that is even more invisibly connected.

When you start developing experiences where people collaborate with robots, you can see robots as interfaces, similar to how web browsers provide a "screen" to the Internet.

Instead of being physically present yourself at some place, a robot can interact or capture information on your behalf. This goes beyond 90s-era webcams, to the traffic information streamed to your smartphone that enables you to use live data to find the shortest path to your destination. Or the robots around the world that record and track weather information across the globe.

Some argue that the extent to which connected robots have already changed our lives makes us as humans more "cyborg" (cybernetic organism) than pure human (see Figure 14-1).

Figure 14-1. Transforming into cyborgs (photo credit: Amber Case, http://caseor ganic.com)

It is hard to imagine modern life without the connected robotic technologies that enable it. From our smartphones, to our laptops, to the many connected devices that surround us, we depend on technology for communication, collaboration, and knowledge. This idea is promulgated and explored under the term *cyborg anthropology*, which you can read about at *http://cyborganthropology.com/Main_Page*.

Positive Versus Negative Views on Cybernetics

In the 1940s, the scientist Norbert Wiener defined cybernetics as "the scientific study of control and communication in the animal and the machine." Still today, feedback and control systems are heavily based on information. Information leads to more accurate pictures of the world.

Cybernetics, cyborgs, and robots have been explored in science fiction, representing both positive and negative views on the world. The positive ones are utopias (for an example, read the first part of Bruce Sterling's novel, *The Caryatids*), the negatives are called dystopias (for an example, read Dave Eggers's novel *The Circle*, or George Orwell's *1984*). Both visions display the great power of collected information. Whether these images are hopes or fears depends on how the humans in the novels access and act upon the information available.

Extending your senses through a few robots is just the beginning. From this foundation will emerge the possibility of interaction between hundreds or thousands of devices that may help us to find lost items, track patients in hospitals, improve transport, or enhance food production on farms. Enabling robots to connect and interact with one another can lead to enormous systems.

Connected Products

Imagine inputs from tiny robots collecting data of all sorts, from all sorts of places, and storing it for tracking, analytics, and ad targeting. In its most extreme expression, this is the vision of the IoT as a web of data and devices, resulting in complete information about our world.

Besides capturing data (inputs from devices and robots), the IoT provides new systems for "outputs," tailored experiences of your environment.

One example of this is the weather clock tempescope (*http://www.tempescope.com/connected*), which visualizes weather forecasts from the Internet.

Figure 14-2. The tempescope™ weather clock, created by Ken Kawamoto

Another example might be a drone that knows how to avoid obstacles as identified by an online database.

Products with Internet access will shape new kinds of homes too (Amazon Dash buttons come to mind). The smart home will include devices that sense everything from who should and should not be present on the premises to the number of eggs in the refrigerator—and does something about it.

Responsive Environments

New kinds of environments can bring intangible information to life as physical objects in the environment. A simple conception of this is the buzz and ding of your phone when you receive a text message, a notification, or a new retweet. Another example is the Doppel watch, a new kind of wristband as shown in Figure 14-3. The watch sends a rhythmic pulse to your wrist to mimic a heartbeat-like sensation. The effect could be calming or enlivening, similar to listening to music.

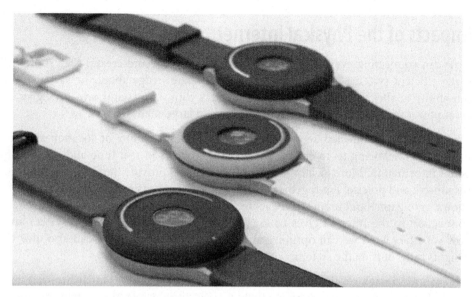

Figure 14-3. The Doppel watch (http://www.doppel.london)

Connecting personal environments and contexts would not only be interesting for economic purposes, but also for political and artistic purposes. One project by maker/artist Bilal Ghalib made the tragedy of war visceral with Internet-connected bracelets. A brief flash of heat would encircle your wrist when a bombing occurred, hopefully inspiring you to perform peaceful acts.

Environments with inputs and outputs also influence the design of journeys within spaces. Not so long ago, you would navigate in a city or country with the help of paper maps. Modern maps are embedded in their environments themselves. For example, in ski areas or event arenas, there are environments that respond to data from sensors and can use LEDs to show on a laser-cut map which of the local ski routes or paths are suggested in real time.

In addition, information can be broadcast about particular spaces. For example, in a museum, an app might send you information about particular paintings you have viewed during the course of your visit.

Another nice example based on Bluetooth is the Tile device (*https://www.theti leapp.com*). With Tile, you can easily detect where you put your car, a bag, or your keys in the range of 20–50 meters.

Impacts of the Physical Internet

How can connecting everything change the way we work and create? Our ability to make efficient systems hinges on two things: our knowledge about the system, and our ability to alter that system. Robots, as devices with sensors and actuators, give us great power to learn about and direct the course of large-scale systems.

More localized connected *sensors* means a higher resolution of location-specific information, allowing us to create more complete maps in real time and work with better information. More localized connected *actuators* provide the ability to be more responsive and precise. Put together, a network of many sensing and actuating robots allows us to gather and immediately act on information in many places at once. Their connection to the Internet gives us logging as a bonus: insight into the system and how we affect it, so we can optimize and improve. The connection can also give us insights from outside the system.

For example, imagine a field of food crops. The status quo is to standardize watering across large areas, usually without much specific insight into the system. But now imagine that there are hundreds of soil moisture sensors evenly distributed across the field. These can report back the soil moisture as a map of which areas might be under- or overwatered. Over time, they can also provide a farmer with knowledge of seasonal patterns specific to the land.

Imagine now that the distributed connected robots have not just sensors on them, but sprinkler heads. Instead of just providing the farmer with information, the robots (complete with actuators) can regulate the watering in-time and in-place according to set parameters. This lets you produce crops more effectively with less runoff.

Finally, imagine these sensing, actuating, crop-watering robots not just regulating and reporting back, but leveraging inputs from outside the system. The robots are connected to the Internet, and so have access to weather APIs. Because of this, robots can use the prescience of meteorologists to make smart decisions on how to act, rather than using only regionalized data about the soil's current state. If it will rain tomorrow, the sprinkler heads could be programmed not to go off, even in dry areas.

We now have much more information about the system, performing more optimally in terms of regulating plant needs, and we are using our water resources more efficiently.

The example can be further expanded: what if the sensors and actuators also worked with pests and pesticides? What about soil acidity? Fertilizer needs?

But expanding beyond the agricultural sphere, similar principles can be applied to many large-scale processes. In a factory, for instance, we have much actuator automation, but rarely do we have good real-time sensory logging. In a warehouse, we traditionally use humans to count inventory, but what if each item in the warehouse already knew what and where it was? That's instant inventory, and a history associated with each item.

There is something wonderful about this technology, but also something frightening. Intelligent monitoring and dispensation of water from hundreds of individual nodes could have a major impact on our water usage. But the energy and materials used to make these hundreds of robots (as well as the waste once the electronics degrade) could also have a major negative environmental impact. And in human-oriented systems, privacy issues are immediately relevant. Where do we find the tipping point in these technologies? As technologists, it is our duty to consider the full impact of the technologies we create, with an eye toward building ethically and sustainably.

## CHAPTER 15

From Products to Toolkits

JavaScript and its libraries are already popular when it comes to building services, APIs, and products on the Web. For example, the jQuery library simplifies many online web browsing experiences. This book sketches how JavaScript has been evolving into hardware and systems for the IoT.

JavaScript as a Toolkit

JavaScript might not be the right tool for every job. But JavaScript and its libraries can be *a toolkit* to connect and prototype hardware devices. As Eric von Hippel notes in his important book *Democratizing Innovation* (MIT Press, 2005):

> Users apply *a toolkit* in conjunction with their rich understanding of their own needs to create a preliminary design, simulate or prototype it, evaluate its functioning in their own use environment, and then iteratively improve it until they are satisfied.

By using JavaScript, people with diverse backgrounds (especially nonengineers) can be empowered to design and prototoype their own hardware. With hardware boards such as Arduino, Intel Edison, or Tessel, users can start to innovate in a much shorter time compared to more "professional" solutions that require vendor-specific programming hardware and compilers.

To help you get a feeling for different aspects of hardware development, Chapters 2, 3, and 4 discussed different "blink" examples. From this experience, more complicated hardware boards (such as boards with embedded Internet that we discussed in Chapters 5 and 6) or different components for physical inputs and outputs (covered in Chapter 7) were explored.

The Power of Modularity

The main power of JavaScript-based toolkits for hardware come from JavaScript modules. Eric von Hippel investigated the nature of good toolkits in detail. He formulates the importance of modules as follows:

> Custom designs seldom are novel in all their parts. Therefore, a library of *standard modules* will be a valuable part of a toolkit for user innovation. Provision of such standard modules enables users to focus their creative work on those aspects of their product or service designs that cannot be implemented via predesigned options.

Node.js is built on the concept of modularity: npm, the Node package manager, is a massive library of tools for the developer. A given tool can be small, but because there are so many of these tools (freely licensed and contributed from thousands of developers), any given project can be much simpler. The smaller problems are abstracted away.

Important examples of JavaScript libraries and modules were discussed in Chapter 8. For example, the Johnny-Five library by Rick Waldron provides abstractions for many boards and components. This library is a good start to build connected systems with JavaScript.

With foundations in hardware and JavaScript libraries for hardware, Chapter 9 looked into the examples of network protocols and JavaScript. Understanding network protocols is an important aspect of building connected devices. Running a web server with Node.js only requires a few lines of code.

What's more, because JavaScript and Node.js are usually used for the web, hardware that can be programmed in JavaScript and Node.js can tie into web-based libraries without additional complexity. Chapter 10 gave examples for web interfaces and Chapter 11 showed how to connect systems with an information "cloud."

Modularity in Hardware

While toolkits in JavaScript empower users to innovate in software, sharing hardware and circuits is still a bit more challenging than sharing code. Open source hardware (OSHW)[1] is not yet as far along as open source software. There are not as many tools available yet for the global community to share their hardware designs, and it is more difficult to turn shared designs into physical hardware. But these tools are in progress, and as they become more popular, the pace of innovation for hardware will increase just as it has with open and modular software.

---

[1] The Open Source Hardware Association (*http://www.oshwa.org*) is working to bring awareness to the movement.

Nathan Seidle, founder of SparkFun, provides a nice overview about the way the Internet revolutionizes hardware development (*https://www.youtube.com/watch? v=xGhj_lLNtd0*). He emphasizes that our work as engineers no longer involves writing patents or preventing others from copying our ideas. In a connected world, our job is making products that sell. At SparkFun, selling is done via the Internet, which means that people also buy "information" and "content." They want to see and understand schematics and board layouts.

The Tessel 2 is an especially interesting example of how a hardware device can link software developers to hardware products. Not only is the board (and the software it runs) open source by design, but it has been designed with open source software toolchains. The Tessel is a strong open source toolkit and module system for IoT products.

Inspired by the same ideas that drive open source software, you can easily extend the Tessel. Once you know the basics of CAD designs for printed circuit boards, you can design and prototype your own Tessel modules. Ordering at companies such as OSH Park, you can start building your own prototype boards for under $10.

Node.js: Driving Innovation in the IoT

We are beginning to see more modularity and sharing in the hardware space, but the progress is slow. Fortunately, we do not have to invent all of the ideas and tools of open source from scratch. Because open source is now widespread in software, we can adapt the tools and lessons from that movement to hardware.

For hardware products, social communities with engineers, designers, and users are still developing. For these information communities, the Internet is critical. These communities can learn from open source software. The open source software movement, often software engineers themselves, have built the tools they needed.

For open source hardware, tools to interact with blueprints and projects online are still developing. To build these tools, software engineers will play an important role, despite being members of a hardware-driven movement. For the movement to progress, software engineers must learn about hardware (likewise, hardware engineers should expand their knowledge of software). People who straddle both worlds are required to build the IoT.

The IoT is exciting to web developers because it gives them new capabilities to interact with the world. And by embedding Node.js, we make the web-to-hardware transition more natural. We create a community with software, hardware, Internet, and open source built in. This is how we create new modular hardware, and how we move the open source movement in the hardware direction.

Node.js doesn't just drive innovation in the IoT. By bringing web developers into the hardware space, the IoT drives innovation in how physical technology is developed.

Building Good Technology

As we stand at the beginning of the physical Internet, it is our responsibility as creators to think deeply about what we are building. It's the second version of the Internet, and you can have a hand in creating it.

As first creators, go out and build—learn what it is to create a new form of industry, one based on responsive human environments. As you progress in this journey, ask yourself: How does this new thing change the human experience? How does it impact the planet as a whole? Am I building technology that creates positive change? Iterate to create the world you hope for.

Node.js

Module Basics

A module is the JavaScript concept of a code library. Modules are good places to collect functions, objects, or ideas that might get reused across different projects. They can help deal with files, data, or communication with external devices.

The Filesystem Module

Suppose you want to open a file and read data. Node.js has no functions for files built-in, but it does have a nice *module* to work with files.

 If you work with Mac OS X or Unix, many embedded devices show up in the filesystem as files under */dev/*. Reading, writing, and controling an embedded device from a host computer has many similarities to reading and writing to files.

To load the filesystem module, you `require` its reference `fs`. This generally looks as follows:

```
var fs = require('fs');
```

By loading the `fs` module, you have access to many objects and classes that help you to work with files in JavaScript.

 Bookmarking the Node.js API documentation is a good idea. The API docs for the filesystem can be found here: *https:// nodejs.org/api/fs.html*.

Let's play with the module in the Node.js console. First, you can open a Node.js console with:

```
$ node
```

Then, you require the module:

```
> var fs = require('fs');
{ Stats: [Function],
  ...
```

As you can see, the JavaScript object `fs` has many functions for working with files.

Within the object's methods, you will find two interesting functions to read a file, both starting with `readFile`:

```
fs.readFile
fs.readFileSync
```

The filesystem module provides both "synchronous" functions and "nonblocking" or "asynchronous" functions. The "sync" version of a function blocks code execution until the file is completely read. This can be useful for reading smaller files where you don't expect a large delay from reading. However, blocking the JavaScript event loop is not nice for other functions. When working with smaller files, reading a file synchronously can be OK as long as you don't expect a large delay from reading.

Besides loading a module with `require`, you can share modules by using the module.exports syntax across different projects.

Writing a module yourself is very simple too. You basically declare what part of code you want to make available to others with:

```
var myFunction = function() {
  console.log('my function');
}
module.exports = myFunction;
```

You could require this module similarly to requiring the filesystem module. Say you have some code to parse a CSV file. A simplified script might look as follows in a file called *parseCSV.js*:

```
var fs = require('fs');

// read a CSV file and return its values
var parseCSV = function(filename) {
  var data = fs.readFileSync(filename);
  return data.toString().split(',');
}
```

Again, the first thing you see in the script is the reference to the filesystem module. Then comes the declaration of a JavaScript function `parseCSV`. Inside this function, we read a file with the synchronous version (when working with small files, this is often the easier approach). Finally, the values from the CSV file are returned.

 Many functions from the fs module, such as readFileSync, return a Node.js "buffer." A buffer is a low-level data type that directly corresponds with raw values in memory and only a minimum amount of encoding information. Later, we will review the use of buffers to communicate with a serial port. Right now, we just need to convert a buffer to a string representation.

To read a file from the command line, you add these lines:

```
var fields = parseCSV(process.argv[2]);
console.log(fields);
```

To test this code, you can run from the command line:

```
$ node parseCSV.js test.csv
[ '10:12', 'greeting', 'hello_world', '1', '88\n' ]
```

Now, to turn this parser into a Node.js module, you can make a module parseCSV that you can require in other places. Therefore, you must explicitly declare what function to export:

```
module.exports = parseCSV;
```

The resulting module *parseCSV.js* file is:

```
var fs = require('fs');

// read a CSV file and return its values
var parseCSV = function(filename) {
  var data = fs.readFileSync(filename);
  return data.toString().split(',');
}
module.exports = parseCSV;
```

The require and module.exports syntax are the basics of working with Node.js modules.

The Node Package Manager

With the npm, you can easily import code that other developers published to the npm website. It is often a good idea to look in the npm repository before reinventing the wheel when you begin a new project.

Install Modules with npm

Working with npm has two aspects: you declare the project's dependencies in a manifest file *package.json* (which can easily be installed with npm), and npm provides some commands to run specific scripts for your project.

Let's start by looking at how to install modules.

A Node project defines its module dependencies in a file called *package.json*. For new projects, you can set up a project manifest with:

```
$ npm init
```

Inside of the *package.json* file, you'll find a number of default settings:

```
{
  "name": "sandbox",
  "version": "1.0.0",
  "description": "",
  "main": "index.js",
  "scripts": {
    "test": "echo \"Error: no test specified\" && exit 1"
  },
  "author": "",
  "license": "ISC",
  "dependencies": {
  }
}
```

To install a module to find different files, you can use the `findit` module by @substack:

```
$ npm install --save serialport
```

The module will be installed in a local folder */node_modules*, and you will see the dependency including its version listed in the *package.json* file.

Running Scripts with npm

In the project manifest *package.json*, there is the possibility to save commands for running scripts. Under a field `scripts`, you can specify a command to execute from the command line. For example, you might want to add a command to check your network connectivity. To do this, you would extend the scripts sections with:

```
"scripts": {
  "ping": "ping npmjs.com"
}
```

The server *npmjs.com* is the address of the npm. You'll find plenty of useful modules there, as you will see in a second. Let's test the new script:

```
$ npm run ping

> serial-test@1.0.0 ping /Users/pmu/projects/node/sandbox
> ping npmjs.com

PING npmjs.com (54.187.170.181): 56 data bytes
64 bytes from 54.187.170.181: icmp_seq=0 ttl=47 time=189.291 ms
64 bytes from 54.187.170.181: icmp_seq=1 ttl=47 time=197.831 ms
```

This looks like a response from a network. You could also test connections to the serial port, list information about serial ports, or upload a default Arduino sketch.

The Stream Module

If you receive data over a network or the serial port, you might not know how much and when data becomes available. Instead of blocking code execution or managing execution threads, Node.js provides streams to solve this problem. With streams, you can observe and manipulate the flow of data over time. A stream is a bit like a river where data "flows."

Streams provide a mechanism to work with chunks of data, whenever data is available.

The simplest stream is a readable stream that emits events when data is read or received. As a first step, let's write a stream that echoes the received data:

```
var fs = require('fs');
// create a stream from a file
var rs = fs.createReadStream('test.csv');

rs.on('data', function(buffer) {
    console.log('stream: ' + buffer.toString());
});
```

What happens is this: we create a data source from reading a file. This stream "rs" will emit a "data" event after reading a line. The received data is a buffer type. We can convert a buffer to a string with `toString()`.

A writable stream executes a `write` function when the Node.js VM allows it to. We add this function to the stream:

```
ws.write = function(data) {
  console.log("input=" + data);
}

ws.end = function(data) {
  console.log("bye");
}
```

Finally, we pipe the input from the command line into the stream with:

```
process.stdin.pipe(ws);
```

 Working with streams is a bit like plumbing sources and sinks for data. For example, you can *pipe* events from the readable stream into a writable stream. "Piping" data from one stream into another, similar to Unix pipes, is one of the advantages of using streams.

A simple test shows how this works:

```
$ node pipe_out.js
hello
input=hello
```

You could also pipe the output of a file into the write stream as follows:

```
$ echo hello | node pipe_out.js
input=hello

bye
```

The command line, requests from networks, and data from the serial port will all be based on streams.

Early Hardware for IoT Systems

Raspberry Pi

The Raspberry Pi is an SBC that was built for students to learn about Linux and pro-gramming. But its goals are more ambitious. Jack Lang, chairman of the Raspberry Pi Foundation, said it like this: "We want to revolutionize the desktop."

To make that happen, the Raspberry Pi iterated a number of revisions. There is the Model 1 and Model 2. Model 1 comes in a version A and B. The differences lie in the amount of RAM, CPU performance, price points, and options for connectvity. For example, while Raspberry Pi Model B allows you to have Ethernet by default, a Rasp-berry Pi Model A needs some workarounds to set up an Internet connection.

One of the most popular variants of the Raspberry Pi is the B+, as shown in Figure B-1. The core of this board is a Broadcom BCM2835 system-on-chip with integrated CPU, GPU, and a USB port. The boards include an SD card slot so you can run Linux from an SD card.

As you can see, the Raspberry Pi form factor is different from an Arduino. Compared to an Arduino, the "Raspi" has an SD card drive, multiple USB ports, a display adapter, and some pins for digital inputs and outputs. The pinout for the Raspi pin headers are found here: *http://pi.gadgetoid.com/pinout*. While an Arduino has digital and analog I/O, the Raspi only has digital pins.

The different form factor is one of the reasons you can't leverage an Arduino project by default on the Raspberry Pi. But besides the difference in physical connections, the system voltage on a Raspberry Pi is 3.3V compared to the 5V of most Arduino boards. This means that you risk destroying your board when connecting 5V compo-nents from an Arduino to a Raspberry Pi.

Figure B-1. The Raspberry Pi B+

Another difference between Raspberry Pi and Arduino is connectivity. The Raspberry Pi supports Ethernet by default. But for WiFi, you must add a WiFi dongle into one of the USB ports.

The default Linux image for the board is a Debian image that you can download here: *https://www.raspberrypi.org/downloads*. "Using Embedded Linux" on page 78 explores the setup of an SD card. It is important to know that as soon as you switch on the device, it loads its operating system from a flash drive.

Once the board has booted, you can log into it with an SSH shell session. Exploring ways to connect is covered in "Network Configuration" on page 81. A nice command to get more information on computing power on a board is:

```
$ cat /proc/cpuinfo
```

Let's continue looking at different hardware setups.

BeagleBone

The BeagleBone project was launched by Texas Instruments, DigiKey, and Element14 in 2008. BeagleBone boards have gone through a number of revisions already.

One of the newest and cheapest is the BeagleBone Black, shown in Figure B-2. The board has an AM335 ARM Cortex A8 processor, 256 MB of RAM, and a clock frequency of 1 GHz. It has 2 GB of onboard flash memory.

Figure B-2. The BeagleBone Black with a WiFi dongle

The board has a number of peripherals, such as a microHDMI connector for video output and an SD card slot for external storage. It has an Ethernet port for easy network connectivity. If you want to use WiFi, you must add a WiFi dongle.

The board comes preloaded with a Debian Linux distribution. BeagleBone Black comes with a JavaScript runtime called BoneScript.

The BeagleBone supports multiple I2C and SPI busses. In contrast to a Raspberry Pi, a BeagleBone has onboard ADC for analog-to-digital conversion.

To get started you can follow the instructions at: *http://beagleboard.org/getting-started*.

Intel Galileo

As you can see from Figure B-3, the Galileo is pin-compatible with an Arduino Uno. This means that the board offers 13 digital pins, 5 analog inputs, a power header, an ICSP header, and a UART port. To connect to networks, you can use the Ethernet interface of the board.

The core of the board is a 32-bit Quark microprocessor, which is a Pentium class microprocessor that runs on 400 MHz and has 256 MB of RAM.

Intel has released two versions of Galileo:

- The Gen 1 board uses a Cinch connector as serial debugging output. You can find adapter cables at SparkFun or on eBay.
- The Gen 2 board provides FTDI header pins for connecting to the board. It also provides a USB Type A connector for peripheral devices.

Figure B-3. Intel Galileo with a Quark SoC 1000

Similar to the Raspberry Pi, the Galileo loads an embedded Linux operating system from an SD card. By default, the Galileo comes with an SPI (serial-peripherial-interface) flash memory with a small Linux distribution preinstalled.

The board schematics are open source and you can download them from here (*http://download.intel.com/support/galileo/sb/galileo_schematic.pdf*). A reference PCB to build your own boards is available for download here (*http://www.intel.com/support/galileo/sb/CS-035279.htm*).

To configure connectivity via Ethernet, you would first log in via the serial terminal. Another option is to use Arduino sketches to obtain basic network settings. The Arduino sketches for Galileo allow you to run Linux commands on the board.

The embedded 8 MB flash memory is too small to run Node.js, and you must run Node.js from an SD card. A number of images are prebuilt.

Index

requesting weather with, 126-130

I

I2C library, 118
iBeacon, 202
IBM Bluemix, 178
IDE (Integrated Development Environment), 25
information communities, 221
instruction sets, 61, 77
integrated circuits, history of, 3
Integrated Development Environment (IDE), 25
Intel Edison, 74-76
    and Poky Linux, 81
    Debian distribution for, 81
    OS downloads, 79
Intel Galileo, 231-232
    for weather station, 140
    OS downloads, 79
Internet of Things (IoT), 1-9
    (see also physical Internet)
    basics, 1-9
    embedded devices, 3
    embedded Internet, 4
    examples and use cases, 7-9
    JavaScript and, 9
    Node.js as driver of innovation, 221
    protocols, 5-7
IP address, 72

J

JavaScript
    and Internet of Things, 9
    and JSON, 13
    as toolkit, 219
    basic syntax, 11
    flexibility of, 1
    for distributed programming, 9-13
    for embedded devices, 16
    for hardware abstraction layer, 106
    higher-level functions, 11
    in browser environment, 13
    objects and arrays, 12
    on servers, 14-16
    programming Arduino with, 30
    runtime environments, 13-17
Johnny-Five library, 107, 114-118
    analog inputs, 117

    and NodeBots community, 185
    board object, 114
    buttons, 116
    empty project creation for, 114
    Nodebot class, 118
    proximity detectors, 117
    REPL setup, 115
jQuery
    adding MVC to interface, 154-157
    user interface with, 152-157
JSON (JavaScript Object Notation), 13
jumper wires, 103
JXCore, 17

K

kernel, 80
Kilby, Jack, 3
Knex, 134

L

Lang, Jack, 229
LEDs
    blinking, 21
    for prototyping, 96
Lee, Thomas, 190
LibMRAA library, 107, 119-122
    communications, 122
    interrupts, 121
    MRAA setup, 119
    outputs, 120
    reading inputs, 120
libraries, Node.js
    Cylon.js library, 122
    for hardware, 105-123
    I2C library, 118
    JavaScript for hardware abstraction layer, 106
    Johnny-Five library, 114-118
    LibMRAA library, 119-122
    node-serialport library, 108-114
Linino, 80
links, 5
Linksys, 80
Linux
    embedded (see embedded Linux)
    NodeRED and, 179
loop() function, 26
Lua, 16

About the Authors

Patrick Mulder has an MSc from Eindhoven University of Technology (NL) and worked in different technology companies focusing on embedded systems, web interfaces, and measurement systems. In addition, Patrick is the author of *Full Stack Web Development with Backbone.js* (O'Reilly, 2014). Patrick runs the Arduino meetup in Munich (*http://meetup.com/Munchen-Arduino-Meetup*) and shares thoughts online at his blog: *http://thinkingonthinking.com*. He likes to travel, to prototype ideas, and to solder.

Kelsey Breseman is an engineer and Steering Committee member of the Tessel Project—an open source organization whose aim is to empower web developers to enter the connected-devices space. Previously, Kelsey has been involved in developing consumer drones, research on sleep and temperature, implantable vision devices, and devices for lung cancer diagnosis. She has a degree in neural engineering, and is interested in prosthetics, speculative fiction, circus arts, and really long walks.

Colophon

The animal on the cover of *Node.js for Embedded Systems* is a common cuckoo (*Cuculus canorus*).

The cuckoo family gets its common name and genus name by onomatopoeia for the call of the male common cuckoo. In France, for example, it is known as the coucou, in Holland koekoek, in Germany kuckuk, in Russia kukush-ka and in Japan kak-ko.

Common cuckoos spend their winters in West Africa and in the spring they migrate 10,000 miles north to England. They inhabit various types of countryside, including woodland margins, open farmland, hedgerows, and marshes. They feed on the ground and are one of the few British birds to relish hairy caterpillars. They also eat grasshoppers, flies, beetles, and small snails.

The cuckoo's life strategy is built on deceiving other birds. The cuckoo is well known as a brood parasite because it tricks other birds to raise its young, allowing for more cuckoos to be reared than would otherwise be possible. Cuckoos can adapt different plumage patterns to match a local bird of prey; a deliberate ruse to frighten small birds away from their nests. The hen cuckoo flies to an unattended nest and lays one egg. The cuckoo egg mimics the color and shape of the host egg, except the cuckoo egg has a thicker shell and a shorter incubation time. The cuckoo chick hatches first and wiggles around the nest, ejecting the host eggs. The chick needs the same amount of food as a whole brood of nestlings so to compensate for the visual stimulus of just one gape, the chick makes rapid begging calls that sound like an entire brood. Many hosts have evolved defenses against these tactics but both sides are fighting to get the upper hand. This behavior is a vivid demonstration of evolution: for every stage that the parasite tries to deceive the host, the host evolves at that stage.

Many of the animals on O'Reilly covers are endangered; all of them are important to the world. To learn more about how you can help, go to *animals.oreilly.com*.

The cover image is from Lydekker's *Royal Natural History*. The cover fonts are URW Typewriter and Guardian Sans. The text font is Adobe Minion Pro; the heading font is Adobe Myriad Condensed; and the code font is Dalton Maag's Ubuntu Mono.

Get even more for your money.

Join the O'Reilly Community, and register the O'Reilly books you own. It's free, and you'll get:

- $4.99 ebook upgrade offer
- 40% upgrade offer on O'Reilly print books
- Membership discounts on books and events
- Free lifetime updates to ebooks and videos
- Multiple ebook formats, DRM FREE
- Participation in the O'Reilly community
- Newsletters
- Account management
- 100% Satisfaction Guarantee

Signing up is easy:

1. Go to: oreilly.com/go/register
2. Create an O'Reilly login.
3. Provide your address.
4. Register your books.

Note: English-language books only

To order books online:
oreilly.com/store

For questions about products or an order:
orders@oreilly.com

To sign up to get topic-specific email announcements and/or news about upcoming books, conferences, special offers, and new technologies:
elists@oreilly.com

For technical questions about book content:
booktech@oreilly.com

To submit new book proposals to our editors:
proposals@oreilly.com

O'Reilly books are available in multiple DRM-free ebook formats. For more information:
oreilly.com/ebooks

O'REILLY®

Learn from experts.
Find the answers you need.

Sign up for a **10-day free trial** to get **unlimited access** to all of the content on Safari, including Learning Paths, interactive tutorials, and curated playlists that draw from thousands of ebooks and training videos on a wide range of topics, including data, design, DevOps, management, business—and much more.

Start your free trial at:

oreilly.com/safari

(No credit card required.)